CW00675797

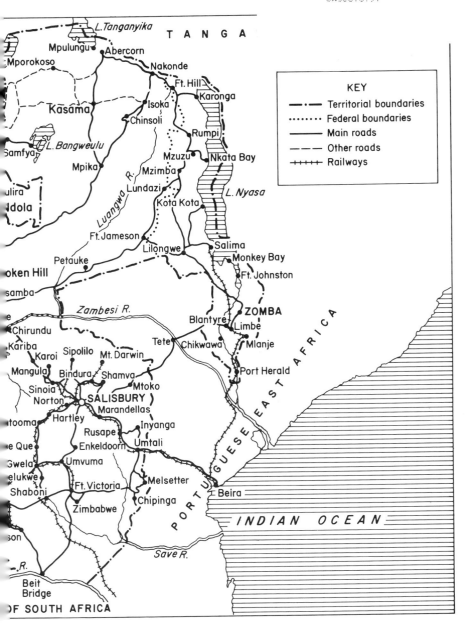

L. Tanganyika

T A N G A

Mpulungu • Abercorn

Mporokoso

Nakonde

Ft. Hill

Karonga

Kasama

Isoka

Chinsoli

Rumpi

L. Bangweulu

Samfya

Mzuzu • Nkata Bay

Mpika

Mzimba

Lundazi

L. Nyasa

ulira

Kota Kota

Idola

Ft. Jameson

Lilongwe

Salima

Petauke

Monkey Bay

oken Hill

Ft. Johnston

samba

Zambesi R.

ZOMBA

Blantyre

Limbe

Chirundu

Tete

Chikwawa

Mlanje

Kariba

Karoi

Sipolilo

Mt. Darwin

Mangula

Bindura

Shamva

Port Herald

Sinoia

Mtoko

Norton

SALISBURY

Marandellas

tooma

Hartley

Inyanga

Rusape

e Que

Enkeldoorn

Umtali

Gwela

Umvuma

elukwe

Ft. Victoria

Melsetter

Shaboni

Beira

Zimbabwe

Chipinga

P O R T U G U E S E   E A S T   A F R I C A

son

I N D I A N   O C E A N

R.

Save R.

Beit
Bridge

F SOUTH AFRICA

KEY

—·— Territorial boundaries
········ Federal boundaries
——— Main roads
– – – Other roads
+++++ Railways

AFRICAN EXPERIENCE

AFRICAN EXPERIENCE

*An Education Officer
in Northern Rhodesia
(Zambia)*

T. E. DORMAN

The Radcliffe Press
London · New York

Published in 1993 by
The Radcliffe Press
45 Bloomsbury Square
London WC1A 2HY

175 Fifth Avenue
New York
NY 10010

In the United States of America
and Canada distributed by
St Martin's Press
175 Fifth Avenue
New York
NY 10010

Copyright © 1993 by T. E. Dorman

All rights reserved. Except for brief quotations in a
review, this book, or any part thereof, must not be
reproduced in any form without permission in writing
from the publisher.

A CIP record for this book is available from the British Library

A full CIP record is available from the Library of Congress

ISBN 1-85043-568-5

Printed and bound in Great Britain by
WBC Ltd, Bridgend, Mid Glamorgan

Contents

General Foreword to the Series

Awhole generation has passed, nearer two in the case of the Asian sub-continent, since Britain's colonial territories in South-East Asia, Africa and the Caribbean achieved independence. In the Pacific the transfer of power came about a decade later. There was little interest in recording the official or the personal experience of empire either in the inter-war years – viewed by some, often among those personally involved, as the apogee of the British empire – or in the immediate aftermath of empire. And in this latter period attitudes were critical, largely condemnatory and even purposively hostile. This is not surprising: such a reaction is usual at the end of a remarkable period of history.

With the passing of time and with longer historical perspective it was possible to see events in a better and more objective light and the trend was gradually reversed. In due course there came about a more sympathetic interest in the colonial period, by those in Britain or in the countries of the former empire who were intrigued to know how colonial government operated – in local, everyday practice, as well as at the policy level of the Colonial Office and Government House. Furthermore, those who had themselves been an integral part of the process wanted to record the experience before, in the nature of things, it was too late. Here was a potentially rich vein of knowledge and personal experience for specialist academic historians as well as the general reader.

Leaving aside the extensive academic analysis of the end of empire, the revival of interest in the colonial period in this country may be said to have been stimulated by creative literature. In the late 1960s there were novels, films, radio and TV programmes now and again tinged with a touch of nineteenth-century romance and with just a whiff of nostalgia to soften the sharp realism of the colonial encounter. The focus was primarily on India and the post-1947 imagery of the 'Raj': there were outstanding novels by Paul Scott – surely destined to be one of the greatest twentiety-century novelists – J. G. Farrell and John Masters. Later appeared epic films like *A Passage to India* and *Gandhi*, the charming and moving vignette of *Staying On*, and, for Africa, *Out of Africa* and *Mister Johnson*.

In the second half of the 1970s there emerged a highly successful genre of collective 'colonial' memoirs of the *Tales of* . . . format: Charles Allen's splendid trilogy *Plain Tales from the Raj* (1975), *Tales from the Dark Continent* (1979) and *Tales from the South China Seas* (1983), followed by others like *Tales of Paradise: Memories of the British in the South Pacific* (1986) and *Tales of Empire: the British in the Middle East* (1989) – all good history and good reading.

Throughout the period from India's independence until that of the last crown colony there had, of course, been those splendid works which combined academic history and creative literature: for example, Philip Woodruff's *The Men Who Ruled India: The Founders* (1953) and *The Guardians* (1954); and Jan Morris's *Heaven's Command, Pax Britannica* and *Farewell the Trumpets* (1973–8).

Finally, as the 1970s gave way to the 1980s, those voices which had remained largely silent since the end of empire now wanted to be heard. The one-time colonial officials, be they district officers, agriculturists, veterinaries, medical or forestry officers, policemen or magistrates, and just as often their wives, began to write about their experiences. They wrote with relish and enthusiasm, with a touch of adventure and few personal regrets. There was a common feeling of a practical and useful task well done, although some thought that more could have been achieved had independence come about more slowly.

These memoirs often began as little more than a private record for the family, children and grandchildren, some of whom had never seen a colonial governor in full fig, shaken hands with an emir or paramount chief, discussed plans with a peasant or local politician, or known at first hand the difference between an *askari* and *alkali*, an *amah* and an *ayah*.

By 1990 the colonial memoir had begun to establish itself as a literary genre in its own right.

Foreword

The initiative of the Radcliffe Press in harnessing and promoting this talent, primarily autobiographical but also biographical, promises to be a positive addition to both the historical and literary scenes. Here is a voice from the last Colonial Service generation, relating from personal experience the lives and careers involved in the exercise of latter-day empire. They were part of what was arguably the most influential and far-reaching international event of the second half of the twentieth century, namely the end of empire and the consequent emergence of the independent nations of the Third World. It could perhaps also be argued that this is part of an even greater process – decolonisation 'writ large', a sea-change in world affairs affecting greater and lesser powers into the late twentieth century.

It may well be that by 2066, the centenary of the closing down of the Colonial Office, great-great-grandchildren will find the most telling image of Britain's third and final empire in these authentic memoirs and biographical studies, rather than in the weightier imperial archives at the Public Record Office at Kew or in Rhodes House Library, Oxford.

A.H.M. Kirk-Greene, lecturer in the Modern History of Africa, University of Oxford, and formerly of the Colonial Administration Service, Nigeria.

1

The Long Road to Africa

It is only comparatively recently that the world has become as small as it is. Before World War II, if you lived in Australia or New Zealand, 'down under' as people often used to say, you really were a long way from the rest of the old Western world, from Europe, from the British Isles, which were frequently referred to as 'home' in Australasia, even by people who had never been there. You were a long way off in time as well as in distance. At that time air services were still little past the experimental stage; the normal way of taking a 'trip home' was by ship through the Panama Canal or the Mediterranean, or round the Cape of Good Hope, a journey that took a minimum of five weeks and sometimes as much as seven or eight. Actually it was usually a pleasant and relaxed way of travelling, for the world was not then obsessed with speed as it is now, speed largely for the sake of speed and not because you really gain anything by it. It usually results in a period of physical and mental exhaustion, often spoiling the first day or two of a holiday when you get to the other end. In those days you were resigned to the slower speed of everything and I do not think I am alone in saying that the world was perhaps a better place for it. Australia and New Zealand were the remote Antipodes, the other side and the other end of the world, and neither end really knew a great deal about the other. Even today, amid the deafening roar of jets and the mad hustle to get around the world, a lot of people still think New Zealand is part of Australia and cannot grasp that the two countries are more than a thousand miles apart. It used to take three and a half days to get from one to the other; now it takes an hour or two.

1

Contemplating seeing something more of the world from a place like New Zealand was quite a daunting prospect. You needed time and money, and the latter, especially, was not easy to come by in the 1930s. I was lucky in a sense that, having been born in England, I had had a taste of travelling fairly early in life, while not yet old enough to be able to appreciate what I experienced. My father, who was the export manager for a large firm of wholesale stationers in London, was sent out to Melbourne in 1926 as their first Australasian representative to establish the firm in that part of the world. We all moved away from England in October of 1926 to spend the next two years in Melbourne, but in 1928 my father, having visited New Zealand in the course of his work, decided to move to another promising new land and set up on his own there as a bookseller. So in the last weeks of 1928 we sailed from Melbourne to Bluff and from the end of that year New Zealand became our home. I reached the age of fifteen a short time after our arrival in Invercargill. By the time we settled in New Zealand I had seen a bit of the world: the Canary Islands; Cape Town; Fremantle and Perth; Melbourne and some of Victoria; and then a glimpse of Milford Sound, when we entered it and spent an hour or two there on our way to Bluff. Incidentally, we travelled on the 'Manuka', which about a year later on a similar trip from Melbourne to New Zealand struck rocks and sank off the Otago coast. I suppose that first taste of travelling stirred my interest in other places and other people, and I never lost my desire to see a little more of the world.

The years that followed were, of course, the years of the depression. Somehow my father managed to keep his head above water, though only just, and the business survived to become a very well-known bookshop in Invercargill for almost thirty years. When my father retired, he handed the shop over to my younger brother, who sold it shortly afterwards in Invercargill, but retained the name of the business, opening anew in Christchurch, where he carried on until he in turn retired. Meanwhile, my elder brother and I worked with my father for a time in the shop, but we both had our eyes on other things. With the depression sitting hard on everyone, there was no chance of our going to university as we had hoped, at least not at that stage, so we studied as external students, something quite a number of people did during those bad years. My brother actually succeeded in completing his B.A., but I stopped short after two successful years because I secured a job on the *Southland Times*, a job that involved working all night as a proof-reader and doing some reporting by day as well. It was work I liked, but unfortunately it gave me eye trouble and after two years I had to leave the job, turning then to what had originally been my second choice of career after journalism, teaching. From the beginning of 1937, until I finally retired at the end of 1982, I was involved in education, as a teacher, as an inspector, and as an administrator. However, four years of war service came out of that, from the end of 1941 until the beginning of 1946, service that brought me into contact with members of the colonial service in which I had been interested ever since I left school. In fact, while studying externally, I had made contact with the Dominion Liaison Officer for the colonial service in Wellington, a very lofty English gentleman, who obviously thought I was mad even to enquire. I mean, chaps with Rhodes Scholar qualifications had been turned down, what! And I, dash it all, I hadn't even been to a public school! As far as I was concerned then, and still am now, Southland Boys' High School could hold its head high alongside any other school anywhere. That response from Wellington never put me off. I think it just made me determined that one day I would get into the colonial service.

My years at the Dunedin Teachers' College were combined with university work and I was able to complete my B.A. degree. In those days the teacher's course was usually two years, but I was lucky enough to be awarded a third year as a specialist in experimental education, an interesting period of concentrated work on intelligence and vocational testing that was to stand me in good stead in later years in Cyprus, in Africa, and in Western Samoa. My elder brother also appeared on the scene, at Selwyn College, to take his theological course for the Anglican priesthood and to gain a master's degree in history, so we both eventually got to Otago University. Meanwhile, the war had broken out in 1939, but I found myself among the rejects, having been told that I could not see well enough for any of the services. I kept trying and had the distinction, if it can be called that, of being turned down no

3

less than eight times. Towards the end of 1940, I secured a post at Scots College in Wellington, moved there as a housemaster, and transferred my studies to Victoria University, where I began work on a master's degree in English. As I had a full schedule of work and house duties at the school, my English professor advised me to spread my M.A. over two years, so 1941 became my first year, which I successfully completed. Meanwhile, the war went on and not so successfully at that stage. Regular call-ups were now in force and my name duly came up in August 1941.

This time, according to officialdom, I could see much better than before. I could be taken into the army, though they doubted that I would ever get overseas. I was organised to move into camp, but I slid down a shale face on a cross-country run and broke four bones in my foot, so that put me out again for some weeks. Then came 7 December 1941, and attitudes – and physical standards! – changed. Miraculously I could see perfectly well and by the first week in February 1942 I was in camp at Porirua. My army career had begun. By September 1942 I was in the O.C.T.U. at Trentham, a course I went through very successfully, and by March 1943 I was in Fiji, seconded to the Fiji regiment, later moving off with them into the Solomon Islands to fight the Japanese. Meanwhile my young brother was entering his fourth year with the Fleet Air Arm on the other side of the world. It seemed that our family had got itself into a traditional English pattern, even if it was only for the period of the war, one son in the navy, one in the army, and one in the church.

I spent a very interesting three years with the Fiji Regiment, a period during which inevitably we did a lot of training and waiting and a lot of fighting in a comparatively short time. I finished the war as a captain and the Adjutant of the Third Battalion and came back to New Zealand to become a civilian once again, but in many ways a different man. I had had a fuller contact with the outside world at a much more mature age and one thing it did for me was to make me fully a New Zealander. Our family, like many others of similar background, had clung to its land of origin, probably helped to do so by the attitude of so many New Zealanders in those days to what they called 'home'. My war years took me out of the New Zealand environment even more than might have been

4

the case had I gone to the Middle East to the New Zealand division there. I was with troops of another race and working with brother officers of widely different origins. I think this made me realise that I no longer belonged to England and Ireland, but to New Zealand where my roots had now gone down.

At the end of January 1946 I was demobilised from the army, (incidentally, being solemnly told that I was not really a Grade I man because of my astigmatic eyes). Those concerned were quite hurt when I roared with laughter at this piece of information. In the final months back in Fiji, when we were being geared up to go off to Burma, something the atomic bombs stopped for us, I met up again with a lady I had known at the Dunedin Teachers' College. We became engaged before leaving Fiji, and were married back in New Zealand early in January in Gore, the service being conducted by my elder brother. I resumed work at Scots College in Wellington and we lived for that year of 1946 in Island Bay, where my wife also taught. It was a busy life and we enjoyed it, but we both had an urge to move on and experience more of the world. Even before I left the army, I had again instituted enquiries about the colonial service. This time New Zealand had a very different Dominion Liaison Officer, a pleasant, friendly, encouraging man, and I also had the backing of my former commanding officer, a man who had now served in both world wars as well as in the Indian army for years.

By the time I had made formal application to join the service, attitudes to recruitment had undergone very considerable changes. 'Colonials' were looked on with much more favour, even though they might not sport an old school tie! About the middle of the year, I was called for interview by the New Zealand selection board, a body of nine distinguished figures under the chairmanship of the governor-general, who then happened to be Sir Bernard Freyberg. Among the nine members was the New Zealand Director of Education. I duly appeared, along with, I believe, sixteen others, at Government House and, when my turn came, sat on a very isolated chair in the centre of a very large room to face a semi-circle of board members. Most of them had some questions to ask, but Sir Bernard, hard soldier as he was, had a facility for putting you at ease. He had also taken the trouble to read up on the Fiji Regiment and its doings and, as far as I could make out, had my military record in front of him. The interview was not easy, but I felt it had gone well and I was not disappointed. A few weeks later I was informed that I had been accepted, and not long after that I was offered a job in Cyprus as a master at the English school, a day and boarding establishment for Greek, Turkish and Armenian boys in the capital, Nicosia; a job in the education branch of the service. I had to finish out the year at Scots College and then there were some problems with shipping – it seemed a lot of people wanted to move round just after the war – but eventually we sailed from Wellington on 11 May 1947 en route to our first tour of duty.

As this book is meant to deal with Africa and our years there, it is not appropriate to go into much detail about our time in Cyprus, but I must make a few comments because the years in Cyprus gave us our first experience of life in the colonial service, enabling us to see its good and its not-so-good features. I say that because, no matter what happened, there were no really bad features. The unpleasant things, when they did occur, usually seemed to be tempered or balanced by something much more pleasant.

Cyprus was a fascinating place historically and, of course, politically. It was alive with history, Greek monuments, Roman monuments, Crusader fortresses, Venetian palaces and castles, Turkish adaptations, and two major languages, Greek and Turkish, two systems of education, two kinds of heritage and culture, both of them deep-rooted. Our major task in education was to see that both systems maintained a good standard and, where possible, to link the two in a rather vain endeavour to produce Cypriots rather than Greeks and Turks. With a fierce nationalism on both sides there was not really any great chance of success. We saw the rivalry and antagonism from the moment of arrival, for the English school was ethnically mixed by design, with English as the main medium of instruction. After two years teaching at the school, the last few months as the deputy principal, I was moved to education headquarters as an inspector and administrator, work that enabled me to see a lot of Cyprus, meet a lot of the ordinary people, and gain a good understanding of its problems. These were the days of the Enosis movement, union with Greece, even though everyone knew Greece did not want Cyprus. The movement was a political weapon for both Cyprus and Greece, however. The trouble and the murdering, what we now call terrorism, had not yet begun, and fortunately we were away from Cyprus before it did. We spent seven years on the island and enjoyed it, but in the end I worked out that four people would have to move away or die before I could keep progressing, so I made an application for a transfer.

Things like transfers always take a long time and the Colonial Office always moved with a deliberate and dignified speed. No undue haste or emotion must be shown, so months passed without a sound, but, as it happened, we were due for our second leave in 1953 and this time planned to go to England instead of home to New Zealand, as we had done in 1950. Apart from a brief couple of days in London and a train journey to Liverpool in 1947 to catch the boat to Egypt, Hazel had never seen Britain and I had not been there for twenty-seven years. Despite having two small children to look after by that time, we had a good, interesting leave and in the course of it I got myself to the Colonial Office. A very polite and smooth young man there was amazed to find I had not yet been told that four posts were available, one in the Far East and three in Africa. We discussed these and I eventually picked the post in Northern Rhodesia, the territory that became Zambia on its independence in 1964. We went back to Cyprus after leave, knowing that we would soon be on the move again, an exciting and yet in some ways a sad prospect, for we had made many good friends in Cyprus: British, Greek, Turkish and Armenian. Yet we knew it was time to move on for people like ourselves with a young family. We, who were working in Cyprus, could see what was coming and what it might mean, much as we had grown to love the island and its people, whatever race they might be.

One of the great dates in our lives seems to be 9 January. We were married on 9 January 1946. On 9 January 1950 our daughter, Rosalind, was born in Nicosia Hospital – with snow on the ground and oranges on the trees! On 9 January 1954 we left Cyprus for Africa. And much later, on 9 January 1971, we celebrated twenty-five years of marriage on the day that Rosalind became twenty-one. But the occasion that is most relevant to this story at the moment is that of 9 January 1954.

We were up very early that day, an exciting one for the children, who were not affected by departure the way we were. Our plane took off at seven in very clear weather, so we had a splendid trip across the Mediterranean and down Egypt to Cairo. As we knew the chief pilot, we all went into the control cabin in turn to look down on the sea and the Nile delta and the desert. We spent the morning in Cairo looking around, but could not go very far with children aged four and not quite three. By midday we were on the train for Port Said, a trip full of interest for us as well as for the children, especially when we came within sight of the Canal and could see ships apparently sailing through the sand!

Rather surprisingly we reached Port Said on time, and were soon established in the Casino Palace Hotel, though we had the usual delays with couriers and the cashing of travellers' cheques. The weather was actually cold and windy by that time, as Egypt can be in the winter, so we were glad to get indoors and stay there. Rosalind celebrated her fourth birthday in our large hotel room, with a cake made by Cyprus friends and carried over in the plane, complete with candles. That birthday has always stayed in the memory of all of us. A couple of days later we boarded the boat that was to take us down East Africa, but only after a day of minor upheaval. It appeared that my courier had cashed travellers' cheques for me not at Thomas Cook's as I had told him to do, but with an illegal street operator. I went off with an Egyptian customs officer to find and identify the courier, a two-hour business that fortunately ended successfully when I was able to identify him. We then all went off to find the street operator, which took another hour. Eventually everything was sorted out, both the courier and the street operator being sent off with fleas in their ears after a lot of shouting in Arabic and table-thumping. I was very glad to see the end of all this, as I knew no Arabic and did not know exactly what was going on. We finally got on board the ship, the 'Leicestershire', just after seven in the evening and sailed late that night. There were only fifty-four passengers on board and just ten of these, ourselves included, were destined for the full length of the trip, ending at Beira in Mozambique.

Travelling on what was primarily a cargo boat, we had numerous ports of call: Port Sudan, Aden, Mombasa, Tanga, Dar-es-Salaam,

Zanzibar, Lindi, Mtwara and finally Beira. During the journey we actually spent three weeks in Mombasa; there was a lot of cargo to load and unload. Moreover, the larger mail boats had a priority at the wharves, so each time one came in we had to move out into the harbour until it had departed, and then go back in again to carry on with unloading. We learned a lot about Mombasa, the town, the harbour, and some of the surrounding country. A trip to Shiwo-ta-Lewa, some miles inland, gave us our first taste of Africa's corrugated roads as we rattled along, sometimes travelling almost sideways. Later we became hardened to this form of travel, but at this stage, after the narrow but quite well-surfaced roads of Cyprus, it was a startling experience.

Our stays in other ports were short, sometimes only a day. Zanzibar was memorable first of all for the fact that you could smell it well before you could see it. The smell was pleasant, full of the richness of what grew there, in particular the cloves. The city itself looked astonishingly clean with its white buildings and narrow streets, though it was not quite so clean when you saw it at close quarters. Dar-es-Salaam was very attractive and very tropical in appearance and atmosphere. But one of the most interesting places was Mtwara, established from nothing as a port for the famous – or infamous – groundnut scheme that was such an ill-advised and ill-prepared project. Mtwara had a magnificent natural harbour and was supplied with wharves and massive storage buildings, but behind it, where there should have been a thriving town, there was virtually nothing; it was a port with no proper hinterland because the scheme that was supposed to utilise it never really developed at all.

The end of the journey for us, and the turn-around point for the ship, was Beira in Mozambique, then still Portuguese territory, an unusual place which was attractive in its way. It was built largely on sand and at one time boasted a tramway that ran on rails just laid on the surface and undulating with the sand, moving when the sand moved. However, that had gone when we passed through Beira, and the roads and the railway were rather more firmly established. But we still had another interesting little experience to face as an introduction to railway travel in the more southerly part of Africa. We had heard of the Mozambique railway, which was not exactly noted for its efficiency, but we boarded the train to find a well-appointed, clean compartment and a generally pleasant and obliging staff. Beira and much of Mozambique is hot and humid, as we quickly found out, but the train was air-conditioned and felt quite pleasant. The night, however, proved a trial. We grew cooler and cooler and drew blankets over us. Then we grew hotter and hotter and still hotter, throwing all our covers off again. This alternating pattern went on and on. Eventually I went out to investigate and found a rather sleepy attendant who spoke some English, so I was able to find out what the problem was. The air-conditioning would not work automatically, so he sat by a switch. When he thought the coach was cold enough, he switched off; when it warmed up again, he switched on. Unfortunately between each switching he fell asleep, until either the cold or the heat woke him up again! He was a cheerful, obliging fellow and there was nothing I could do; he was at least doing his best. We parted happily and I went back to endure the rest of the night with the family. We woke up next morning to find ourselves almost into Umtali, having climbed up from the humid, thickly covered coastal strip to the high country of the African plateau in what was then Southern Rhodesia. Our first act when the train stopped was to walk in the cool, clean, fresh air, a remarkable change from the night before. Umtali was a pleasant introduction to Central Africa and we wondered how Northern Rhodesian towns would compare. We were not to be disappointed.

Southern Rhodesia, later to become Rhodesia and then Zimbabwe, is a comparatively open country compared with the territories further north and in some respects is not unlike New Zealand, a point that struck us immediately. We now changed to Rhodesia Railways, which proved far more efficient and reliable; a dining car was added to the train and we moved on steadily and comfortably all day, reaching Salisbury at about six in the evening and staying there for a two-hour break, so we were able to go out and walk around the town. It was more than just a town, but like a New Zealand city, colourful and sprawling. Some years later we had a holiday there and were able to explore it thoroughly; this first visit was just a glimpse, but a pleasant one. But I think it was then that we really realised we would not see the sea again for about three years.

It was already dark when we left Salisbury, which has now, of course, become Harare, the name of its main African suburb. Fresh air and the break we had taken there soon put the children to sleep – and us! When we woke up again we were very nearly at Bulawayo, where we were due to stay one night in a hotel. We had two full days there, finding it an attractive place, which for some reason reminded us of Oamaru, despite the fact that it was so far from the sea. One of the striking features was the jacaranda, which was all in bloom and very colourful. After the restrictions of ship and train, we were all glad to walk about as much as we could before moving off on the final stage to our new home, Northern Rhodesia.

The entry into Northern Rhodesia was, and still is, the bridge across the Zambesi at the Victoria Falls, the first sight of which we got from the train as we rolled slowly across the bridge, high above the gorge and the turbulent water. Above the falls the river is the best part of a mile wide; below them it is something like a couple of hundred yards. That first glimpse, even through the spray and from a moving train, was most impressive. It even reduced our two small children to silence for a few moments! That night we paused for about twenty minutes at Lusaka, the capital city of our new territory, just long enough to have a few minutes with friends from Cyprus who had been transferred here not long before us. Then we were off again in the darkness en route for the Copperbelt and Ndola, which was to be home for us. The next morning, dull, warm and sticky at first, but later much clearer, saw us run into our final station. It was 1 March 1954, nearly two months since we had flown out of Cyprus, but three weeks of that had been spent in Mombasa. There was a great sense of relief that we had accomplished the journey, by air, by sea, on land, with so few problems; we had for the most part actually enjoyed the trip and, travelling as we did on a cargo boat, we had seen places that the usual traveller down the east coast did not see at all.

Once we left the ship and began our train journey inland, we very quickly realised how great was the contrast between Cyprus and Africa beyond the Sahara. Cyprus was hot and dry most of the time with a short, very cold winter, so it had sparse vegetation, its forest areas largely man-made and controlled, the whole island small and compact. The Africa we now saw around us was miles and miles of trees with comparatively few open areas, unlike Southern Rhodesia, for here, further to the north, we were on the edge of the real Central Africa, the land of rain forest and red earth, a place of vast distances, where, as we soon discovered, you could travel many miles without seeing much, if anything, of man and his works, only the primitive land with its natural foliage and its wildlife. In a straight line we were now six hundred miles from the sea at its nearest point. We were about thirteen degrees south of the equator. Cyprus had been a little over a hundred miles long and only fifty miles wide at its widest point, approximately thirty-five degrees north of the equator. You could get to every corner of Cyprus. In Africa there was more than room to move around; there was room to get well and truly lost. Cyprus showed its history in the works of man over many centuries. Africa concealed its history in its vastness, and man was insignificant, making no more than little scratches here and there on the surface. Much as he would like to be the master, man is still only scratching the surface of Africa, still really rather insignificant in many ways. And more often than not, when he does do something, he spoils what is already there, things that have been there for centuries. Africans themselves do this just as much as Europeans, though perhaps we opened the door for them.

In Cyprus we had been in part of the cradle of Western civilisation and there was plenty of evidence of the centuries of development. For the most part the environment was tamed and controlled. Man was more or less the master. Looking at the Africa we had just entered, we saw a land that was not mastered, a land where man still struggled to make his mark at all. There was no developed civilisation here as we knew it. Despite the veneer that was visible in towns like Ndola, the Africans, the indigenous people, were still living from hand to mouth, by hunting and by subsistence agriculture.

This was the impression we had from the moment of our arrival and the years that followed only reinforced it. Our job was to help prepare Africans to take over their own country and to run it without the need for massive aid. The colonial service had a great measure of success in bringing that about, despite the fact that the time available was drastically cut short in the face of political pressure. In our world you cannot do without politics and, inefficient as it is in many respects, democracy is the best system that has evolved so far. No doubt the time will come when Africans in all the various territories scattered over that huge continent will evolve out of dictatorship. At present they are living through a period that the more developed world endured mainly in the seventeenth and eighteenth centuries; we are in fact still growing out of it and the overall evolutionary process has taken us the best part of a thousand years. The Africans are trying to cover the same ground in about a hundred years.

Ndola and the Copperbelt gave us our first taste of life among Africans, people who had a different culture and who were behind us in what is termed 'development', unlike the Greeks and the Turks of Cyprus, whose culture and development were similar to our own and just as advanced. Later we experienced other areas of this part of Africa, some much more remote, different tribes, different outlooks. Like us, Africans can be very different even within the same country, something we learned to understand and appreciate more and more as time went on. Understanding takes time and I felt I was really just beginning to understand Africans fully when the time came for us to leave the territory. Perhaps this is something many so-called 'experts' of three weeks' sojourn in a country could realise a good deal more than they do.

I suppose we could say that 1 March 1954 was the end of our road to Africa. Now we had arrived, new people with a young family in a new land. We had our first impressions and we felt the impact of change to a vastly different world. We were now looking ahead to what lay in store for us, the adapting to new conditions, different people, the problems of establishing ourselves in our surroundings, of getting to know and work with another set of colleagues. Ahead, too, lay the understanding and appreciation of Africa and some of its people, eleven years of hard work, minor triumphs, frustrations, and through it all the development of our family. Looking back, we can see that they were interesting years, good years, years of achievement in our work and in ourselves.

2

Northern Rhodesia and Zambia

In 1964 Northern Rhodesia, the Crown protectorate, became independent Zambia, a new state in complete control of its own affairs. It was the culmination of an intended progression, though that culmination came rather earlier than was originally intended and perhaps before the country was really ready for independence. But in the latter half of the twentieth century this has invariably been the pattern, as former colonies struggled to achieve self-rule.

Until about the end of the eighteenth century, central Africa, what used to be called 'darkest Africa', was practically unknown to Europeans. The north and north-west coasts had become increasingly familiar to European explorers and adventurers since the days of Christ. In the great days of exploration at the time of the Renaissance, knowledge of Africa extended further and further south until, by the end of the fifteenth century, Europeans rounded the Cape and found their way up the east coast to India and the distant East, the Spice Islands – the area Columbus thought he had reached when he discovered the West Indies in 1492, unaware of the huge American continent that lay between him and his goal.

Penetration of the African interior began as early as the sixteenth century, but the hard-headed and practical Portuguese and Dutch were interested in its commercial possibilities, its resources and its potential for trade, not in exploration for the advancement of knowledge. When exploration yielded no practical results, they turned aside from that area and went elsewhere. Those who went into the vast regions beyond the coastal strip, climbing up to the plateau, found a maze of tribal lands and tribal divisions, and struggles for power there, just as in the 'civilised' world to which they belonged; empires built up and controlled by force, and just as quickly destroyed by force. For thousands of years one branch of primitive man had developed there, completely isolated from those who had developed in the Euphrates area and in the far interior of China. The early so-called Bantu people, developing into more and more tribes and sub-tribes as they grew in number over the centuries, gradually spread west and south-west and south, apparently from the Congo basin. They moved into what became Northern and Southern Rhodesia and Nyasaland (and later Zambia, Zimbabwe, and Malawi) in waves over centuries, waves that may have begun as early as 300 BC. It is known for certain from pottery recovered that Bantu people had penetrated the edge of the area by 90 AD, when far to the north the Roman Empire was approaching its zenith. Movement further south was slow. Southern Rhodesia was entered by way of the lakes and the Rift Valley and showed considerable settlement by 1000 AD. From that penetration developed the Monomotapa empire which reached its height in the fourteenth and fifteenth centuries. The Zimbabwe ruins give us some idea of how great that development was: there is nothing else like it south of the Sahara and Egypt. No Northern Rhodesian tribe ever reached that level.

It appears that the real invasion of Northern Rhodesia, an invasion for conquest, began in the sixteenth century, the invaders following the valleys of the Zambesi and the Luangwa. It is clear that by 1740 the Bemba tribes had fully established themselves and held north-eastern Rhodesia as their homeland. The nineteenth century was the time of European invasion, but it was not an invasion of conquest. Missionary explorers like Livingstone were the ones who penetrated the new lands, seeking to open up the country and extend into it their particular presentations of the word of God. It was a new phenomenon to the Africans they encountered. Some Africans welcomed them as harmless curiosities; some were suspicious, looking for what lay behind the word of God they propounded, unable to believe that this was not just a new approach to conquest and subjugation. In the early stages European governments were not very interested. They did not want further responsibilities and, in Britain's case, the memories of the American Revolution of 1776 were still relatively fresh, where a former colony had risen up against its founders and set itself up as a new independent state. Only slowly and reluctantly was Britain edged into taking any responsibility for Northern Rhodesia. However, once all the European powers began to lay claim to pieces of Africa in what came to be known as the scramble for Africa, Britain wanted her share of the prestige, the resources, and the power that colonies offered a state. At that early stage, no one saw such possessions as land and people to be developed, but only as sources of raw materials, or as military bases. The missionaries alone saw the people, but even they viewed them only as children to be tutored and converted to the service of Christianity, as presented to them by their European fathers and masters. Some of the missionaries never grew out of this attitude and in some places it was still evident in the 1950s and 1960s.

The earliest European explorers and settlers saw the Africa they began to open up to the rest of the world as people as well as land. In West Africa, which had been opened up to the white man for very much longer, the lucrative slave trade had made Europeans see Africans as a commodity rather than as human beings. In Central Africa it was the Arabs who operated the slave trade; the Europeans were already past that stage. However, because they began to penetrate the area during the industrial revolution, they tended to concentrate on what the land itself could offer them in raw materials and resources rather than on the human beings who lived there. Many modern critics fail to understand that this attitude of pure exploitation and profit had already passed before the end of the nineteenth century, and no longer had the same dominance when the twentieth century began. Africans were now seen as people, 'primitive' in comparison with the 'civilised' world perhaps, but people to be traded with, raised to a higher level, and no longer on a par with animals. Livingstone himself had realised this, and quickly appreciated that Africans differed from tribe to tribe and region to region just as Europeans do. He recognised, for example, the quality of the Lozi people: on his journeys from coast to coast through Africa, they formed his staple body of helpers, and it was they who brought his body back to his own people.

16

Rhodes did not see the Africans in quite such human terms, but, in his endeavours to build British influence and a British corridor of land from the south to the north of Africa, he treated Africans as people to be met and reasoned with, people to reach agreements with, to be persuaded, and, if necessary, to be fought. The British South Africa Company, like most earlier administering powers or bodies, tended to treat Africans as children, but the days of blankets and beads were well past and the fact that tribes and their chiefs could have power and dignity was recognised and utilised. Livingstone looked at Africans as a doctor, a scientist, and a missionary, and saw its people as potential Christians who could spread civilisation as Europeans saw it. Rhodes looked at Africa from a political and commercial viewpoint, and saw its people as workers in the building of an empire, workers who would gradually be raised to the level which he regarded as civilised.

In 1890 a conference was held in Brussels on the subject of Africa, still 'darkest Africa' to many peoples and powers. The conference was attended by all the colonial powers from the oldest, like Portugal, to the newest, like Germany, and also included representatives from the United States, Turkey and Persia. As with all conferences, a lot of talk took place, a great deal of it aimed at creating an impression on the international stage or in each home country, but some general lines of agreement emerged. All those attending would police their colonial territories as far as was possible, establish communications, fight slavery, protect the missions operating there, and encourage trade and development. The idea of a sort of trusteeship existed; it was a short step from there to protectorates and Crown colonies. Even in 1890, ultimate independence was there in the back of some minds at the conference, although, if it had been voiced, most people would have laughed at it. But interest in Africa grew steadily, and Central Africa, having only just been opened up to the rest of the world, attracted a lot of attention.

In 1891 the British South Africa Company made a formal agreement with the British government to subsidise a police force for the area south of Lake Tanganyika and for Nyasaland. This area did not include Barotseland, which had its own treaty with the British Crown. At this stage, the company area north of

17

the Zambesi was often referred to as Zambezia or Northern Zambezia. By 1896, the company forces had driven out Arab traders and para-military forces and had extended their power right across the Bemba country. Thereafter Arab power was confined to the coast. From 1891 onwards, missions played a big part in the development of Rhodesia in general, but most especially in the north-eastern area controlled by the company. The White Fathers, Catholic missionaries, were very much in evidence between 1891 and 1899, dabbling in power politics on a small scale as well as saving souls. I suppose the Roman Catholic church has always been the most politically attuned branch of the Christian church and has usually had the personnel and the money to make its presence felt. The British government, while wanting a hand in what went on in Central Africa, was still reluctant to take control completely. From 1898, closer controls were imposed on the B.S.A. Company, the agent of the Crown, so, in that rather devious way that often irritated foreign powers, Britain gradually tightened its grip on Central Africa while still having the company to use as a scapegoat if necessary. In 1897 a form of civil service was established under the company name, which set a course for progression to the top positions, this being designed to stop forceful young men bouncing to the top too quickly. This suited the ideas of men like Rhodes himself, so the company made no serious objection to the scheme. Efficient young men could still progress rapidly enough to satisfy themselves and their sponsors, but slowly enough not to upset the conservative elements of the old school.

Among the striking figures who made a permanent impression on British Central Africa was Robert Codrington, an Englishman of good education and background, who had joined the Bechuanaland Border Police and had served in the Matabele War. By 1895 he had joined the administrative service in Nyasaland as a collector of revenue. Meeting Rhodes in England in 1897, he made an immediate impression and by 1898 he was the Deputy Administrator for North-Eastern Rhodesia in the B.S.A. Company service, at first resident in Blantyre in Nyasaland. Not long afterward he moved his headquarters to Chief Kapatamoyo's village and established what was to become the town of Fort

18

Jameson. In August 1900, he was made Administrator of North-Eastern Rhodesia. He made a point of selecting as his recruits and juniors young graduates from England, a practice that became normal colonial service procedure, and by 1901 he had set up a properly graded civil service in the territory. A contrast quickly became apparent between the administrative outlooks in North-Western and North-Eastern Rhodesia. The North-West tended to recruit locally within Africa, using Europeans from Southern Rhodesia and South Africa, with little regard to background, as long as they had experience of the African land and some of its people. The North-East, on the other hand, sought its officers new from Britain, with good academic backgrounds. To offset their lack of experience of the land and its people, far more native African personnel were used. Both systems seemed to work and generally work well. By 1914 the whole of Rhodesia under the B.S.A. Company was covered by a network of administrative stations, operating with the full consent of the British government, who had what they seemed to desire at the time: extensive indirect control without full responsibility. A look at most colonial service records, no matter for what territory, will show that men like Codrington kept turning up at intervals. The chief difference between the early days of the century and more modern times was that, as the colonial service grew beyond mere administration into a vast service of specialist departments, these outstanding men did not stand out so prominently. Doing a good job at the right time always meant a great deal, but could not attract the same attention in a far larger service of much wider scope.

Taxes were levied in Rhodesia from 1900 in the North-Eastern area and from 1901 in the North-Western, though in the latter region they were not actually collected until 1904. It was easy to collect taxes from tribes with a strong organisation, such as the Bemba; not nearly so easy from those with a much looser organisation. It is interesting to note that the introduction of taxation gave great impetus to migration for work; men wanted to earn money on a more regular basis to pay their taxes. Mine work was becoming available all over Africa below the equator and the mining companies soon built up an organisation to provide themselves with regular labour – and in the early days, of course,

African labour was cheap. By comparison with some other parts of the world it still is today. By 1903, a native labour bureau was established in Southern Rhodesia and it quickly extended its operations further north. At first, Kimberley, Katanga and Southern Rhodesia were the main areas, but it was not long before a regular flow of Northern Rhodesia labour was going to the Rand and Johannesburg. Despite anti-South African posturing, this still goes on today. Without this outlet, which African governments desperately try to conceal, Zambia for one would have a far greater unemployment problem than she already has. During our time in Barotseland in the late 1950s, W.N.L.A., the Witwatersrand Native Labour Association, known colloquially as 'Wenela', had a full-time representative in Mongu and ran its own Dakota planes, regularly carrying Africans back and forth to South Africa. Men usually went on a two-year contract, at the end of which they were flown home again with a lump sum of money set aside from their pay during the period of contract. Many Africans went back on contract again and again. Mineral development in the Rhodesias also led to an influx of settlers from 1900 onwards, especially in Northern Rhodesia after the opening up of the Copperbelt area.

The imperial government was slow to encourage white settlement in Northern Rhodesia. For a long time the Zambesi was regarded as the 'natural boundary' of British Africa and it took Rhodes and the B.S.A. Company a lot of work to persuade Britain that this need not be the case. From its early days the company gave encouragement to farmers; most of the earliest farmers were Afrikaners from South Africa, perhaps still hoping to escape the net of the British government and seeing the B.S.A. Company as something apart, more in touch with the Europeans born and brought up in Africa. The first step on the road to modern Zambia, however, can be regarded as the amalgamation of North-Eastern and North-Western Rhodesia in 1911 into one unit, Northern Rhodesia, still under the B.S.A. Company. Livingstone became the first capital of the new amalgamated territory. Probably many of the European settlers did not realise to what extent the company was the agent of the British Crown and how Britain was gradually, if still reluctantly, tightening its grip on this part of central Africa.

The outbreak of war in 1914 seemed, rather surprisingly, to catch the Northern Rhodesian administration quite unprepared, though with German colonies on their north-eastern border, they should have been well aware of what might happen. Perhaps the main feature of the war for Northern Rhodesia was the fact that no tribe made any attempt to rise up against the British, as at least some of the Germans seemed to think they would. About forty per cent of the Europeans and thirty per cent of the eligible Africans served in the armed forces, and the foundation was also laid for an even greater African contribution when the Second World War came around. The First World War took its toll in Africa as everywhere else, and by 1920 the B.S.A. Company was looking for a way to rid itself of a costly administration and responsibilities that were growing steadily wider. It was still essentially a commercial venture and did not want to get drawn ever deeper into the realm of politics, especially international politics. Britain, interested as she was in the development of the whole Rhodesian area, was still reluctant to take over and set up new colonial territories. A lot of discussion went on, more or less behind the scenes. Inclusion of both Northern and Southern Rhodesia in South Africa was discussed. The amalgamation of Northern Rhodesia and Nyasaland with East Africa was considered. Finally, a plebiscite was held in Southern Rhodesia in 1923, as a result of which that territory became a self-governing colony, annexed to the Crown, with the B.S.A. Company retaining its mineral rights. The British government then agreed to take over the administration of Northern Rhodesia in 1924, the territory becoming a British protectorate, run exactly as a normal Crown colony. (Census figures of the time show that there were then still barely 4,000 Europeans in Northern Rhodesia.) And so Britain at last took responsibility for Northern Rhodesia, a new addition to the list of colonies and protectorates when there was still a British Empire and Britain, despite the ravages and the changes wrought by World War I, was still a power in the world. The colonial and imperial attitude had already changed, however, and from the moment Northern Rhodesia became part of the Empire it was already marked for ultimate self-government and full independence. As early as 1924, new entrants to the colonial

21

service and its younger staff were thinking in terms of moving towards the handing over of power, although at that time most of them were probably thinking of independence within a time-scale of eighty, rather than forty, years.

Northern Rhodesia, then as now, depended heavily on minerals and on copper in particular. From 1922, the mining industry had entered a period of redevelopment, with the B.S.A. Company selling off rights and land concessions to big international companies. From this time, the Anglo-American Corporation and the Rhodesian Selection Trust became powers in the land. Farming grew only slowly, the British government not really being interested in its development until after World War II. It is interesting to note that in the early 1920s segregation of black and white was seriously considered and was one reason for the formation of native reserves. Colonial rule brought in the practice of indirect rule rather than direct control on the South African pattern. This had its problems as well as its advantages. Tribal rivalries remained strong and the European administrators had to tread carefully; jealousies could quickly develop and the obvious scapegoat for the cause of trouble became the government and the European generally. Witchcraft was rife and African myths and superstitions retained a firm hold on the majority of the African population, something that has changed little even today. One example of this was the Banyama myth in the late 1920s and early 1930s. The Banyama were mythical Africans who haunted the bush in darkness, killing people and using their blood and brains for ritual purposes. The myth seems to have arisen in Tanganyika, but by 1929 had appeared among the Bemba and in the northern and eastern provinces of Northern Rhodesia. In Tanganyika the finger had been pointed at the game department, probably because its rangers often had to work in the bush at night. In Northern Rhodesia the belief quickly took hold that Europeans controlled the Banyama and used them to remove people who had offended them in some way. As ritual murders were common amid the already established witchcraft of centuries, the Banyama myth was readily believed by the ordinary village African. The Watch Tower, that rather strange missionary group which still operates round the world, made use of the myth, often subversively, and from it arose several unofficial

22

groups under its name that used the myth as a cloak for nefarious and murderous operations. Witchcraft is a deep part of much African culture, and I shall dwell more on this and my experiences of it in a later section.

The idea of consolidating the central African area was already there in European minds and had been since the scramble for Africa began in the late years of the nineteenth century. In the years leading up to World War II it appeared more definitely and openly, with numerous attempts being made to give it some practical form. The ultimate result was the Federation, but by the time that arrived the chance of true consolidation had already been lost. The name of Moffat in Southern Rhodesia was closely linked with consolidation and he brought the matter up in 1925, but he envisaged rule from his own Southern territory. Settlers in the commercial world and, of course, the mining companies opposed this, though quite a lot of the farming community seemed to be in favour of it. In 1928 a Royal Commission produced definite recommendations, which included the division of Northern Rhodesia. The north-eastern region was to join with Nyasaland. The central and southern line of rail areas, which included the mines, were to become part of Southern Rhodesia. Barotseland was to be a separate native reserve and state on its own. This was discussed, but no agreement could be reached and the idea fell by the wayside. Looking back on it later, it was fairly obvious that it would not have worked satisfactorily. It would have strengthened Southern Rhodesia, but the whole scheme seemed to be built on a European viewpoint and tended to disregard what Africans might feel and think. It also seemed to ignore the idea of eventual independence.

The year 1930 saw an unofficial conference of parliamentarians from both Northern and Southern Rhodesia, but their conclusion was that no amalgamation was possible until the development in the north had reached a level much nearer to that in the south. The British government then shelved the matter; in any case the conference had been unofficial. In 1934 the B.S.A. Company suggested a British Central Africa block, perhaps the first real signs of the federal solution, but the idea of amalgamation of the Northern and the Southern territories was still pursued vigorously, especially from the Southern end by Godfrey Huggins. At about the same time, interest in South Africa began to turn to the idea of a Central African block and by 1936 this line of thought was being quite strongly promoted. In the two Rhodesias further unofficial, and then governors', conferences were held. In 1937 the Bledisloe Commission met, taking its name from its chairman, Lord Bledisloe, who was of interest to New Zealand and New Zealanders because he had been governor-general there from 1930 to 1935. The Bledisloe Commission produced an exhaustive report, the chairman being a man of experience in such work; and was the first body to consider fully the views of Africans as well as Europeans. The conclusion reached was against amalgamation and against federation, largely because of the disparity between the two Rhodesian territories, more or less supporting the ideas of the unofficial conference of 1930. The Commission's ideas were still being digested, when a situation arose that put everything back on the shelf again. The Second World War broke out.

Once again Northern Rhodesia was ill-prepared for war; too much of the Chamberlain outlook had permeated the colonial administration. However, as in Britain and elsewhere, the two Rhodesias soon collected their wits and were on the move quite quickly. The Northern Rhodesia Regiment was formed in 1940 and by the end of 1945 had seen service and action in Somaliland, Ethiopia and Burma, performing well as part of the East African forces. War shed a new light on the African, just as it did on the Fijian in the Pacific, and earned him far greater notice and respect from the European. It became obvious that, trained fully and carefully, he could do far more than most Europeans imagined. It was also obvious that, if he could do this in war, he could do it in peace-time also. The idea of independence suddenly loomed larger and nearer.

After the war came to an end in 1945, the British Empire as such ceased to exist. The rush for independence began and the Commonwealth emerged, with things moving too fast and too far, leaving a vacuum which the Communists attempted to fill. Sometimes we in the colonial service wondered if this speed of events stemmed from the eagerness of Africans to take over their own countries or from the British government's desire to unload an empire that was no longer possible to operate. The two new superpowers, the United States and the USSR, both sought indirect control and influence in all the new states in Africa, without the responsibility of being officially accountable. The Soviets had an ideological commitment to Communism and its spread throughout the world; the Americans were keenly aware of the commercial possibilities for the dollar that lay in the emerging nations.

Post-war development was rapid in Northern Rhodesia and began to concentrate on the advancement of the African far more than ever before. African unions and union representation appeared and progressed quickly. Attempts were made to diversify the economy, to look beyond copper mining, although the mining boom greatly helped the territory's economic and employment prospects. The importance of farming was at last recognised, and for the first time tourism began to enter the economic picture, especially in the game reserves. Out of all this a new class of Africans developed: more affluent, better educated, and, naturally, more anxious to play a real part in the running of their country. It was really this new class and this new attitude of mind that made the Federation something that could not last very long, even before it had started, but at that time few recognised the signs or fully realised what was happening. Only on looking back later did it become obvious.

3

The Copperbelt Days

Zambia, formerly Northern Rhodesia, is a very new country from a white man's viewpoint, even newer than New Zealand and Australia. Until Europeans arrived there with the firm intention of staying, there were no towns as we understand them. Apart from some of the missions, there were really no established settlements, other than the African villages, before 1900, although the first European settlers were gradually moving up from the south and acquiring land to work. Some of these early figures became well known to European and African alike. Perhaps one of the best known, an assistant collector for the British South Africa Company, was J. E. Stephenson, soon known to everyone as Chirupula. His name appears frequently in early records and has a particular connection with Ndola, since he was the one who first pinpointed the site back in 1904 as the best place for an administrative headquarters for the area.

Copper had been discovered in 1903 at a place called Bwana Mkubwa, about five miles from the site of Ndola, but the discovery was not exploited until 1912. The copper mine there had a short life. There was good development at first and steady production until 1930, when the world-wide depression took its toll, as it did in innumerable mines all over the world. Bwana Mkubwa closed down in 1931, and when fuller development later came to Northern Rhodesia's copper, the great centres were further north. In fact, the Ndola area came to be regarded as being just outside the Copperbelt.

The township of Ndola developed slowly and quietly, but steadily. By 1910 there was a population of some sixty white people. As the railway advanced north to serve the copper country and link up with the railway system of the Belgian Congo, Ndola became first a halt on the line and then a station of much more significance. By 1935 it was the main commercial and distribution centre for the whole Copperbelt area. In fact, in 1930, it had been considered as the possible territorial capital, though perhaps not very seriously. Lusaka, some 230 miles further south, was eventually chosen as more central and accessible to the territory as a whole. But, when Northern Rhodesia was organised into provinces, Ndola continued to be the administrative centre for the Western Province, even though Kitwe, the town beside the Nkana mine to the north, was larger. The reason for this was, I think, that the Copperbelt towns – Kitwe, Chingola, Mufulira, Luanshya – all tended to be dominated by the mining element. As everywhere, the big mining companies tended to think of themselves as being a law unto themselves. Very often they toed the government line only with reluctance; people in education encountered this frequently with the African schools in the mine townships. The mine administration sometimes felt – and made it obvious – that we should not be laying down the standards and inspecting the efficiency of what they termed 'their schools'.

In 1954 Ndola was – and no doubt still is – a sprawling town, of the type that used to be referred to as 'frontier' towns. In fact, for quite a long time it was exactly that, for it was the most northerly town in the territory until the Copperbelt area began to be developed further north. The town was close to the Congo border, now the border with Zaire, and it was from Ndola that the railway ran across to link up with the Congo system. The line to Kitwe and Chingola was a branch line that came to an end amid the mines, but was more important to Zambia than the line that carried on over the border. Later it was to make a second link with the Congo system.

The whole area is comparatively flat, although it is four thousand feet above sea level. Apart from where clearances have been made for towns, for roads, for the railway, and for the mining operations, it is all tree-covered, forming the southern boundary of the rain forest that spreads over the whole of Central Africa, stretching out from the Congo River. Living in Ndola, one needed to travel

27

only a mile or two to find oneself looking into the Congo. In fact, one of the large primary schools was so close that a football was often kicked over the border – and retrieved. There were no fences or border guards, only customs and police posts on the roads and the railway. It has to be remembered that the boundaries in Africa were mostly drawn by people in Europe, looking at a map of a vast land most of them had never even seen, who took no note of tribal lands or the traditional African movement about the country. In this part of Northern Rhodesia the indigenous people were mainly Bemba-related, but the border actually placed a large section of them in the Belgian Congo. The border meant little to them and they moved back and forth freely, the administration on both sides having the sense not to erect any barriers, which would have been impossible to maintain and patrol, and would have antagonised thousands of villagers.

Ndola earned a place in aviation history when, in 1920, the first aircraft to fly down into this part of Africa made three landings in Northern Rhodesia: first at Abercorn, near the Tanganyika border; then at Ndola; and then at Livingstone, beside the Victoria Falls. Central Africa is rough country to fly over even now: it must have been far rougher in 1920 with virtually no facilities, no long-range communication, and no ground control; and undertaken in the tiny planes of those days, fragile and unreliable, without all the modern instrumentation that makes flying so safe and accurate in the present day. Many years later, Ndola was again to feature in an aviation event, when, in 1961, the plane carrying Dag Hammarskjold, Secretary General of the United Nations, to a vital conference in the Congo, crashed nearby, killing all on board. This time it was disaster and the air was full of talk of sabotage – a charge that was never really satisfactorily refuted.

Ndola was also notable from its early days for its liberal and friendly white attitude to the African people, with an evident desire to see the Africans as part of the town and not just as a labour force, as was the tendency in the mining towns. Without the magnet of work on the mines, however, not a great number of permanent African residents were attracted to Ndola until after World War II, when an official African township was established in 1946. By 1950 there was some industrial development and the town also became the main centre for the Indian population in the more northerly part of the country, for Indian traders were shut out of the mining towns. The Indians had slowly drifted into Northern Rhodesia over the years from East Africa, where they had first appeared in the nineteenth century as indentured labourers for the cane fields. They also appeared as traders in places like Tanganyika and Kenya. They tended to form much of the trading and commercial element as time went on, especially in Northern Rhodesia, though a few did farm. Their situation was much the same as it was in the Pacific for a long time, but the Indian population in Africa did not seem to expand at quite the same rate as it did in the Pacific islands.

When we arrived in Ndola in 1954, it boasted a population of nearly 70,000, of whom about 7,000 were Europeans. The rest were mainly Bemba-related Africans, so that was the dialect heard for the most part and the one government officers had to learn. The conditions were rather different from those we had experienced in Cyprus, though we still had a long, dry season. Central Africa generally has three seasons: a hot, dry period from September to November; a rainy period from November to April; and the winter, a cooler, dry period from April to September. The temperature pattern was also rather different. The hot season ranged from 80 to 100 degrees Fahrenheit, but because of the altitude never went much over the 100 mark. The cool season ranged from 55 to 75 degrees, although it frequently fell below 50 at night. This was much less extreme than we had experienced in Cyprus, where the summer temperatures often reached 110 degrees, while in the short winter we had snow. There was no snow in Northern Rhodesia. The rainfall was 45 to 50 inches a year, but it all fell in the rainy season spread over only three or four months. The rest of the year was dry and usually cloudless from about July until October, or even November. Over the years we got used to the long rainless period and appreciated it more than we had done in Cyprus, because in Central Africa it was the coolest time of the year.

We were fortunate on our arrival in Ndola because there was a house already vacant, from someone who had just gone on leave. As in New Zealand, every house had a garden area, although I use the phrase 'garden area' advisedly, for many of them had little to show that might be called 'garden'. Rather surprisingly to us, many government officers took the attitude that they were in a particular house for only one tour of duty, usually between two-and-a-half and three years, so there was little point in making a good garden. They kept the grass cut – the garden boy did that anyway – but beyond that did very little. Our building was very new and had housed only one family before us for a little under two years, so the garden was just an expanse of grass – and, in season, mud! The houses themselves were burnt brick with iron roofs in all the larger towns, very much as in New Zealand; so inside we were not plagued with leaks or insects, although there were plenty of the latter about, especially when it was wet and humid. The whole building was wired against mosquitoes. With Hazel on the scene, that bare garden did not last long, for she soon had things growing and beds organised, giving a much more civilised and cheerful look to our surroundings. When the dry season came, there was regular watering to be done, but there was no water supply problem and we could water the garden as much as we wanted.

At first we more or less had to camp in the house, for it took about a month for the rest of our belongings to catch up with us from Beira. The arrival of all our goods made a big difference to our two small children, who had felt a trifle lost without their familiar things around them. We felt a bit the same ourselves, but I had plenty of work to plunge into and was out of the house for much of the day. In some respects, of course, work had to be my major concern, for our life depended on that, so I looked with great interest at what my job as education officer in Northern Rhodesia would involve. In Africa, an education officer had to be rather more versatile than in Cyprus. This was especially true in the more remote areas, but even in a town like Ndola the scope of work had to be wider. I arrived to find myself taking over care of the provincial finance for education, because the accountant was due for leave and there was to be a gap of some weeks before the new man arrived. I pointed out that I had never handled finance on this scale before, but I was told, rather loftily, that 'they had all done this at some time or another'. Being new to the territory, I accepted this – with a large pinch of salt! – and carried on with the job as best I could. However, it did not take me long to find out that what I had been so grandly told was nonsense. No other education officer I could trace had ever been asked to take over the accountant's work as well as his own. Nevertheless, in the long run it did me no harm, for I learned a lot about provincial and territorial finances that stood me in good stead later. Meanwhile it became obvious that no new accountant was really coming, at least not for many months, so I would have to carry on. Actually I carried on until our own accountant returned from his leave in November, rather more than six months from the time he had left his work in my hands.

Despite the pressure of the work, my financial involvement had some lighter moments, one of which came with the annual visit of the auditor. Having learned most of the procedure more or less by trial and error, I had got everything in good order and it all balanced up. I could account for everything, but to the auditor my methods were in some cases, not surprisingly, distinctly unorthodox. He was satisfied that all was in order, but kept eyeing me with considerable puzzlement. He was a quiet little man, who did not say much, but eventually he ventured rather tentatively, 'Tell me, Mr Dorman, how long have you been an accountant?' I could not help laughing outright as I explained that this was the first time I had ever done accounts of this nature in my life. To my surprise, he smiled for the first time and looked relieved. 'Ah,' he said, 'now I understand. I was quite puzzled by some of your procedure!' He was not the only one who had been puzzled; I had had to work out a lot of it for myself. The audit finished up very happily with all in order and with a good report. However, there was a comment to the effect that it was unfair to load education officers with full accounting duties, something for which they were not specially trained, on top of their normal work. I think that probably protected some future officers from what had happened to me.

This unexpected financial work had not been the only source of pressure on me during my first months in Northern Rhodesia. I had another load to carry, although this one was really of my own choosing. For a long time I had been interested in the law at university level. While in the Army I had been involved in several courts martial in both defence and prosecution which had whetted my appetite still further. When I got to Cyprus, I found that London University had its external system in full operation there, so I began a course for Bachelor of Laws. I succeeded in passing the first two stages, but we were transferred to Northern Rhodesia before my final papers came up in June 1954. Fortunately I had kept up my study, even while we travelled down East Africa, and somehow I also managed to continue for those vital last weeks. I was able to sit my finals in Ndola and I was successful, although I did not get the results until November. No sooner had I finished the papers and begun to breathe a little more easily than I suffered an attack of jaundice. I was in bed for a week, extremely sick, with very yellow hands and feet, not to mention the whites of my eyes! When I looked back on my first six months in the territory at the end of 1954, I felt that I could cope with anything. My wife and family must have felt the same.

To me the greatest thing for an education officer to have and to retain is a sense of humour. Fortunately my parents, and especially my Irish father, gave me this. My thoughts on the work of an education officer are perhaps best expressed in an article I wrote a year or two after our arrival in Africa. I have included the article, entitled 'That Education Officer', later in this book. The article was supposed to have been published in the British magazine, *Education*, but I never found out whether it appeared there. In those days one had to get permission for publications such as this, so the article went to education headquarters in Lusaka, where it disappeared into the building that all of us in the provinces knew as the 'Biscuit Factory'. It was lost there for some time, and enquiries I made with the magazine elicited no reply at all. However, I feel the ideas contained in it were true, and, looking back, I believe that they remained true long after I had left Africa, and even to the present day. But back now to 1954.

Once the accountant had returned from his leave and I had finished my Law examinations, I was at last able to concentrate on what I was supposed to be doing: the work of education officer. I was able to get out and about; to meet the teachers, and to visit and inspect the schools under my control. The Ndola district was split in two parts, Urban and Rural, with the latter involving touring out in the bush. Schools were either local education authority (L.E.A.) schools, which were more or less directly government-controlled, or they were mission schools, controlled by a variety of different missions and varying widely in standard. We had to try to raise all schools to a uniform standard: no easy task when some of the missions were desperately short of money. As I saw many different mission schools in different parts of the country, I grew to admire the dedication of some of the missionaries to the daunting tasks they faced, especially as the great majority of mission schools were out in the bush, often hours of driving from the nearest settlement of any size.

Apart from the work that the missions did in the field of education, they were all, of course, also trying to bring the African people into the Christian church – or rather, churches, for each mission naturally presented its own picture of Christianity. I often wondered what the African from a remote village thought, for some of the missionaries condemned one another quite openly. We devised a kind of 'spheres of influence' system for mission schools, more or less laying down areas within which missions could operate their schools. In general this worked fairly successfully and enabled the missionaries to avoid confrontations, not to mention helping to rescue the African villager from yet more confusion about the nature of white man's Christianity. Many Africans regarded it much as they regarded witchcraft, and the missionary was often seen as a sort of witch doctor. Witchcraft was strong, and the further you got from the railway and the main roads, the more powerful it usually became. It interested me, especially when I saw the power it could have and what it could make people do. But I only encountered that power fully later on; the Ndola district, near a fairly large town and on a railway line, was not so subject to the power of the witchdoctor as the more remote areas.

Amid all this activity, our family still managed to get settled into our house. The suburb of Kansenji was quite a long way out from the centre of town, so we needed a car. We acquired a small one which gave us much more freedom to move around. In fact, I frequently used to walk home after work, but I needed transport to get there in the morning, so my wife used to drop me off at the education office. We kept that little car until we went off on leave in 1956, and it gave us good service. We also acquired a kitten, thanks to the veterinary officer, who had become a friend of ours. Our little acquisition soon made himself very much part of the family. We named him Frixos, after a Greek friend of ours in Cyprus. The human Frixos never knew that he had a cat named after him, but I do not think he would have been worried, for the feline Frixos developed into a real character who stayed with us until we left Africa in 1965. We were able to find a good home for him then, keeping in communication afterwards. He was still very much alive some years later, an experienced and much travelled cat within Northern Rhodesia. Our children, now well and truly adult, still remember Frixos and some of his antics. Among other things, he was very good on snakes and helped to keep them away from house and property, wherever we happened to be.

It did not take the European community long to discover that Hazel was a trained teacher, but at that point there were no vacancies in the European school. However, there was a small kindergarten in operation for pre-school children, and the lady who ran it, the wife of an administrative officer, was on the point of going off on leave. Hazel was asked to take over. She did so, and our own two children were added to the group, which met at our own house. It continued very successfully until the end of the year, when the lady who originally ran it returned from leave at the same time as Hazel was offered a post at the European infant school, so Hazel was happy to hand the little kindergarten back to her.

At this stage, it should perhaps be explained that European and African education were separately organised and operated. This was not due to any discrimination or exploitation, but happened for very practical reasons. European children, as elsewhere, were ready to go to school at the age of five, while African children rarely started school until the age of seven, eight, or even nine. This happened because, outside the towns, they often had a long way to walk to get to school; a walk which a child of five or six could not manage. In the course of my time in Northern Rhodesia, I encountered schools where the children walked seven or eight miles there and back to get to school. Clearly, it was impossible to put children of five together in the same class with eight or nine year olds, especially when they came from vastly different backgrounds and often spoke different languages.

In 1953 the Central African Federation had been established, but African education remained under territorial control and was divided into three territories; Northern Rhodesia, Southern Rhodesia, and Nyasaland. This was because of the large numbers of children involved, the tribal differences, and the need for decisions to be taken at a local level which allowed for greater flexibility. European education, on the other hand, was made a Federal concern, for the numbers of children involved were much smaller, and standards at various ages had to be more uniform, so that children could cope when they moved back to a European environment. The long-range plan was to raise the standard of African education to the point where African children could eventually compete on equal terms, especially at secondary level. In my eleven years in Africa, I saw great strides taken in this direction and an enormous improvement in the numbers in schools, in the level of achievement, and in the attitude to the education of girls.

African children generally were eager to get to school and keen to learn, but numbers were so great that coping with them all – and finding the funds for education as well as the other elements of development – presented great problems. All the African primary schools out in the bush, and some of the town schools, ran two sessions a day. One group of children came to school from seven in the morning until about eleven; another then came from midday until about four in the afternoon. The same teachers did all the work, amounting to something like a ten-hour day spent teaching in the school – and I never heard a teacher complain that he or she was in any way overworked! Moreover, it was the Africans themselves who asked for the double sessions.

African children suffered because of the large number of pupils, even though attendance at school was not compulsory. It could not have been, because attendance could never have been checked upon and no system of penalties for non-attendance could have been satisfactorily devised and enforced. But even with voluntary attendance, the numbers who flocked to the schools were extremely difficult to cope with, largely because not enough teachers could be trained quickly to meet demand. Consequently, a scheme had to be devised whereby selection was made at regular intervals throughout a pupil's school life. After the completion of Standard II, only two-thirds of pupils could move up to Standard III. The same thing happened at Standard IV and at Standard VI, and at Form IV in the secondary school. This meant that, by the time a pupil attained Form V, he or she had been selected four times for promotion, so the level of achievement in the top classes of the secondary schools was amazingly high. It also meant, sadly, that some good, solid, hard-working children had their schooling terminated at the top of the primary school or even earlier through no fault of their own. The effects of this severe selection showed up in the public examinations, the British General Certificate of Education, when the results from African secondary schools, especially among the boys, were usually as good as, and sometimes better than, those of the European secondary schools, where a pupil could progress right through the school even though the quality of his work might be very mediocre. It has to be remembered, of course, that African students were older on average by two or three years because they started school much later. This meant that sport between European and African schools was barely possible, because European boys of fifteen and sixteen would have found themselves facing mature, powerful African boys of eighteen or nineteen on, say, the football field. This problem was further exacerbated by the fact that many of the European children came from a South African background, especially in the mining areas. In those days, that meant there could be little contact of any kind, although some gradually began to emerge over the years.

Another problem was the education of girls, for the traditional attitude of the African to girls was that their job was to work in the gardens or the fields, to help prepare the food, to marry and have children, and generally to provide whatever the male might need. For this they had no need of education; it did not even matter if they could not read or write. This attitude was not confined to Africans. Many Europeans shared the same ideas and were very caustic about our efforts to get girls into the schools, while the idea of secondary schools for girls literally horrified some of them.

These attitudes never totally died, but we gradually overcame them sufficiently to get a steady increase in the number of girls in the schools. When I arrived in Northern Rhodesia in 1954, the number of girls in the schools represented barely twenty per cent, mostly at the primary level. When I left in 1965, that percentage had risen to almost fifty per cent, with a significant increase in the number at secondary level (although still small in comparison with the boys).

Not surprisingly, there were no co-educational secondary schools for African children. As it was, pregnancies were fairly frequent, some even in the primary schools, and not always resulting from the attentions of other pupils! I was once faced with the problem of how to deal with a primary school teacher who legally married a girl in Standard IV at his own school. He then wanted her to continue at school, 'perhaps even to the secondary school'. The girl was fourteen, African girls frequently marrying at thirteen or fourteen, and the marriage was all in order and above board, but eventually there was nothing I could do but persuade the teacher to take his new wife away from the school. One of the things I remember most about the event was the consternation of the school's headmaster, who had not been consulted before the marriage took place. He was a staid and reliable man and a very keen churchgoer, so the marriage did not quite fit in with his idea of how things ought to be. He could not really see how such a marriage could be legal – but it was, complete with family agreement, dowry money, and a proper ceremony. In many ways the straightforward cases of sexual interference were much simpler, though sometimes you had to transfer the teacher involved to save his life. It always seemed that mission schools had more sex incidents than local education authority schools, but this was because the moral side of life was, rather naturally, given more prominence in the missions. An African headmaster in a big L.E.A. school once told me, with a very straight face but a twinkle in his eye, that he had few staff problems because 'adultery was easier in L.E.A. schools'. He was probably right to a considerable degree; Africans are realists, living as they do, especially in the bush, close to the land and nature. They are a lot more uninhibited than we are, though once urbanised they tend to fall into the normal pattern of self-restriction, as we all do. In the towns they seemed to lose a lot of their natural sense of humour, though some, like the headmaster just mentioned, managed to retain it.

Once I was freer to move out among the schools and the teachers, I soon began to understand them more fully and found I got on very well with most of them. As in Cyprus, the question of language soon arose. All officers had to become proficient in at least one of the local dialects, which meant passing an examination. Once that had been done, a teacher was supposed to be able to understand what was being said around him, but he could also progress up the salary scale beyond the language bar. One had three years in which to do this, but I was fortunate. I am blessed with a very good ear for languages, as I had already found out with Fijian in the army, and then with Greek and Turkish in Cyprus. At school I had taken French and German, but had little chance even to hear them spoken, let alone to use them. Now I was faced with my first experience of a Bantu dialect, Cibemba (pronounced Chibemba), but having got my Law examinations behind me, I plunged into Bemba classes. The language was an interesting variation from the Latin-based languages, which use endings to deal with plurals and verb tenses. The Bantu languages use prefixes, which was quite a new concept to me. The Bemba people were the Babemba; one person was a Mubemba; the language was Cibemba, and so on. I duly passed my examination in just over a year, but thereafter had the usual experience of European officers trying to learn the African tongue. Since most of the Africans were trying to learn English, if one spoke to a town African in Cibemba, he would answer you in English. It was easier out in the bush where much less English was spoken or heard at all (or much more difficult, according to how one looks at it).

By the end of the year, free of the financial burden of work, I was getting well organised as the district education officer for Ndola, both Urban and Rural. We were getting more settled all round and Hazel got word that she was appointed to the European infant school. As I began to move around the schools, I discovered that most of them had never had a full inspection, so I arranged a schedule of visits for the new term in January. When I began the work, I found that the teachers, though naturally apprehensive about inspection, actually liked the idea and were keen to profit from what they were told. They felt that inspection meant the department and the district education officer had a real interest in them and were trying to help them. It was a good feeling to realise that what I was doing was welcomed and appreciated. I also felt it was a sign that I was reaching the African.

Our first Christmas in Africa was a quiet one, but very pleasant because we felt that we had overcome the trials of change – and surmounted a few other obstacles as well. We hoped there would be at least a year and a half before we went on our first leave from this part of the world, a leave that would take us back to see New Zealand again after a gap of nearly six years. The prospect of steady, settled work for both of us looked good, but, of course, things never work out quite as expected. We had just moved into the new year with plans well laid, when I suddenly got word from the provincial education officer that I was being transferred to Chingola to become the district education officer there, in a Copperbelt area that consisted of two towns, Chingola and Mufulira, each built alongside a massive copper mine. There would be little rural area to deal with. At first, this seemed rather a blow, coming at a time when I was getting to know the Ndola district and the African personnel were getting to know me, but, after I had examined the details of the new district and actually paid a visit to Chingola, we both felt happy about the change. For one thing, of course, it meant I would be out of the provincial headquarters and not have the provincial education officer breathing down my neck all the time. I would have my own offices and staff, my own vehicle, and be able to arrange my movements without constantly having to fit in with someone else. After our initial reservations, we began to see the advantages of the move and started to look forward to it. In any case, we had three months to adjust to the idea, as the move was not to take place until April 1955. Meanwhile things went on as planned in Ndola, my chief regret being that I would miss touring in the bush and the contact with rural Africans – less sophisticated, more dignified, less hurried and more stoical than most of those in the towns.

Chingola was typical of the towns in the mining areas of most of southern Africa. It was modern because it was very new, not having become an established settlement at all until 1943. The war raised the demand for copper dramatically, and many mines and mining towns, closed down and virtually deserted during the 1930s, came to life again in the 1940s, Chingola and Nchanga among them. Previously Chingola had been a rather primitive settlement that merely served the mine, photographs showing that it looked very much like some of the old Australian mining settlements of the last century. The revival of the copper mine brought into being a whole new town, well planned with attractive commercial buildings and good modern housing, both European and African. A great deal of the credit for this went not to the mining company, the huge Anglo-American Corporation, but to a vigorous and concerned town management board that became a municipal council. Chingola gained full municipal status in 1956, its first mayor being installed in 1957.

Like Ndola – and all the towns at this more northerly end of the territory – Chingola was carved out of the endless bush that stretched away into the Belgian Congo. Copper was first discovered in the area in 1924, when a prospector's attention was drawn to an outcrop of rock by a village headman, but no real prospecting was done until 1926. The mining began, but in 1931 the underground workings were flooded and operations were abandoned. They resumed in 1937 when the mine was drained, and mining began again in 1938. Later, in 1957, the huge open-cast mine was developed and the whole mining operation was to become one of the largest and richest in the world. By 1960 some 8,000 people were employed on the mine.

When we arrived in Chingola in April 1955, much of that development was still to come, but Nchanga was already a large and rich underground mine. The town had a population of about 40,000, of whom some 5,000 were Europeans, the great majority of these being employed on the mine, as was also the case with the African population. I had read about the power of the mining companies in Broken Hill in Australia; here I saw for the first time something of that power in a town. The Anglo-American Corporation was very big and very influential in the territory, which I suppose is why I soon detected an attitude of being, if not exactly above the law, then at least capable of bending

40

the law to suit the requirements of the mine and its employees. Fortunately, there were plenty of good men on the administrative side of the mining operations with the good sense and tact to work well with the government and its officers. But there were several occasions when I had to go to the top personnel officers at the mine to sort out problems that arose in the education field because of the attitude of some of the lower-ranked European mine staff, who saw the Africans as labour, men to get the copper out of the ground, and little else.

Our goods were taken up from Ndola in a government truck, but we went in our own little car, along with Frixos the cat and a number of precious breakables. Having travelled a good deal on the roads outside the towns by this time, I knew what those roads were like. The main road was in process of being tar-sealed, but there were still patches of well-corrugated red earth, so we made sure that everything was well packed. We managed the trip without mishap, but the open road was no real place for a small car, heavily loaded, and we were glad to see the end of the journey.

In many ways Chingola made a pleasant change in our lifestyle. The town was well laid out, and more compact than Ndola. The government housing was all quite close to the commercial centre and to the government offices. We lived on the southern side of the town. Beyond that lay the Nchanga Mine African township, while the main African area, Chiwempala, lay to the east of the government offices. At last I could walk wherever I wanted when I wanted. In fact, I soon began to take regular walks and runs and quickly got myself fit again.

In 1954, as already mentioned, I had suffered an attack of jaundice. In the last week of March, 1955, I got the measles! I first had the measles at the age of twenty-four and assumed that I had finished with them, but this, it seemed, was a different variety and here I was with the measles again at forty-one. I was one of those odd people who never got the usual childish complaints as a child; I got them all when I was an adult, except, fortunately, the mumps, which I never had at all. I got over my attack of the measles fairly rapidly and just in time for our move to Chingola in April, but – I suppose inevitably and in a way fortunately – the children caught them from me, first Rosalind just before we left Ndola, then Brennian just after we arrived in our new home. Hazel, having had them as a child, was not affected, but had to cope with us all in turn. For some reason, things like measles never strike everyone at once, but always in succession, so the nursing and the convalescence periods spread over several weeks. Apart from that little happening, which loomed large and unpleasant at the time, our arrival in the Copperbelt proper went smoothly. However, the measles had one lasting effect. Up to that time my hair had been flecked with grey; now I suddenly went very grey indeed. In fact, at first a lot of my hair had fallen out, but it soon grew back as thickly as before – only very, very grey.

For me, the great thing about Chingola was working on my own, being king of my own castle, so to speak. I still had to account for things, but I could plan and stride ahead. I must say that the provincial education officer alongside whom I had worked in Ndola, and who always gave me the impression that he was watching me like a hawk, let me alone to get on with the job once I moved away from his immediate presence. Perhaps it was just a case of 'out of sight, out of mind', or perhaps, after those rather trying first months, he was satisfied that I knew what I was doing. I like to think it was the latter.

I quickly settled down to my two towns and to my large urban schools. The Bemba people still predominated, but the schools contained a high proportion of mine-workers' children, so other tribes were represented, which meant that the usual problems of de-tribalisation tended to occur. Africans removed from their own tribal environment, away from the influence of their headmen and chiefs, frequently found life difficult and the reaction was often violent. Urban Africans tended to drink a good deal – an easy form of recreation common to a great many people of all types and colours – but I felt that these people were drinking simply to get drunk. Naturally, alcohol had the effect of lessening inhibitions, which frequently led to violent behaviour. This could apply to the women as much as to the men.

We were now about seventy miles north west of Ndola. My other main centre of education in the district, Mufulira, was thirty-eight miles east by road, though a good deal less than that in a straight line. A further fourteen miles north-west, a new mine was just opening up called Bancroft, which meant a new African school was opening there also. In the bush areas between these centres there were few villages and no schools, the African children normally walking in to the town schools. I missed my trips out into the bush, but I was kept very busy with my schools, as I found most of them had never been inspected before. Many of the European officers in the African education department got so buried in administration that they neglected the educational side of the work. This was not really surprising, since most of them had a degree but no real teacher training. Their usual background was a degree and a Diploma in Education, which normally meant a one-year course with very little practical classroom work. In other words, many district education officers avoided the inspection side because they did not really know enough about it to feel confident. There were some officers in the department, however, who had full training and good experience, and these took a great interest in the teaching side of the work. One of these was the deputy director of education, who came up to visit the Western Province in September 1955 and showed great interest in the inspection work I had done.

In Chingola I acquired an assistant eduction officer, an African, who proved a great asset. He was intelligent, quick, pleasant in manner, and possessed of a good sense of humour. He was among the first of the growing number of African officers who could meet and mingle with Europeans at their level of sophistication and who quickly won the respect of Europeans and Africans alike. Unfortunately, too many of these men got pushed aside when independence came, by political favourites and the power-hungry. Although he never knew it, my assistant in Chingola served me as a model for a character in a novel I wrote years later, after I had left Africa. I was lucky to encounter and work with a good number of Africans of this calibre in my years in Northern Rhodesia. In fact, things were progressing steadily in the training and development of native Africans, and when I left the Ndola District I handed the work there over to an African officer, promoted to full education officer status. At this stage, especially under the Federation, it was not possible to link up African and European education, something

I felt was a great pity. A lot more could have been done, without actually integrating the schools, to make both sides feel that they belonged to the same system.

Chingola was an interesting social mix, for the town was divided into three groups: the mine Europeans, the government Europeans, and the Africans. Of course, the European staff employed by the mine earned far more than any government officer, and many of them tended to judge status by the size of the salary. In the 1950s, government officers and the commercial fraternity were, in general, regarded more or less as the poor whites of the community. Mining personnel, especially the executive and administrative staff, but even the higher grade underground workers, all made more money than most government officers, and they all seemed to be very conscious of the fact. That never worried most of us, but I once witnessed an extreme case of the difference between the good, intelligent African and the heavy, not very bright European. I was in the district commissioner's office discussing an educational point with a young district officer, when a massive European came in and asked in a thick, guttural South African accent for the papers he had to sign. The D.O. told his African clerk to bring the papers and get the gentleman to sign them, making sure that he witnessed the signature properly. The massive gentleman examined the papers, grunted heavily when the clerk showed him where to sign, and then very laboriously made a cross alongside his typed name. He could not write; perhaps he could read. But the irony came when the African clerk neatly and quickly signed his name underneath as witness, politely thanking the man, who grunted and walked out. The incident was no doubt an extreme case, but it stayed in my mind. I often wonder how far that clerk got in his career in government employment.

Mine and government Europeans mixed quite well socially, but with widely different interests and backgrounds the two groups never got very close to each other. Official functions and sports brought them together, but each group tended to keep to its own for closer friendship. The Africans were in all senses a race apart in the social world. African wives generally had no social life such as Europeans had and rarely accompanied their husbands, even to official functions. They were far behind in their ability to cope with strangers because that was always left to the men. An African woman never appeared, unless called by her husband, and usually, if she were addressed by a visitor, she looked immediately to her husband, who would answer for her. There were, of course, exceptions and, as time went on, the increasing freedom for girls in the schools began to show its effect in everyday life. (Much later I was to be surprised by the very different status of and attitude to women among the Polynesian people in the Pacific; the contrast with the African situation was very marked indeed.)

Life in Chingola was busy, but pleasant for all of us. I had my hands full with my work. Hazel moved from a post at the Ndola infant school pretty well straight to a post at the Helen Waller infant school in Chingola, where Rosalind became a pupil. Brennian went to a pre-school class at the Convent, so we had no problems with looking after the children by day. We were also lucky enough to move into a larger house about a week after our arrival. The only thing missing for me was that contact with the rural African out in his own environment, but, despite that, I got to know Africans more fully and to understand much more of their outlook as time went on. I realised that, as yet, I had not got to know enough about the real Africa, the Africa away from the towns and the veneer of European civilisation. However, one had to know all sides of African life, and this life in a Copperbelt town was part of Northern Rhodesia that I could not miss, if I were to fully understand the country. It was my time in Chingola that gave me an understanding of the South Africans, and the depth and complexity of their problems.

The mines employed many South Africans and, like any other people, they presented extremes. In general, one could say that the Afrikaners, the South Africans of Dutch and French origin, were the ones most difficult for us to deal with in the field of African education. They had their long established background of apartheid, which the most rigid of them based on the Bible. The British South Africans also had their form of apartheid, based on the old colonial outlook, the paternalism that had originated in India and West Africa. It was a looser form of apartheid. I encountered many South Africans in my dealings with the European Education Department, mostly with teachers in the secondary schools, when I was trying to create some sort of link between African and European schools.

One method I tried with some success was to get Europeans to help with the running of African sports, particularly athletics, which was one of my own special interests. I remember especially one occasion when I managed to get two high school teachers, both Afrikaners, to assist as field officials at an African school's sports meeting. One was to run the long jump, and one the high jump, but they were both given African assistants, teachers from African secondary schools. The long jump man, who rejoiced in one of Afrikanerdom's greatest names, Kruger, emerged as a most pleasant, easy man, shaking hands with his African helper on arrival, talking and joking with him all day, and accepting him just as he would any European. The other man was the same age, but dour and rigid. He barely acknowledged his African helper, hardly spoke to him all day, and gave him as little as possible to do. His contribution to a good relationship was negligible. I found the contrast very enlightening – and so did the Africans!

Within a rapidly changing Africa, we carried on our work and our lives in Chingola, learning about the Copperbelt, about the mining community, about European and African education and its problems, and, above all, more and more about the Africans themselves. Our leave came round in August 1956, which meant all the upheaval of packing once again. In the last year before we set off for a spell in New Zealand, we could look back on a lot of incidents, good and bad, but overall the picture was a good one. We had made some very good friends in Chingola and had begun to get closer to the Africans, and to understand them more fully. All sorts of incidents come to mind – our children's enjoyment of the Hippo Pool about twelve miles from Chingola where they swam and had picnics, but naturally never saw a hippo in daylight; the visit of Hillary and Lowe, both New Zealanders, to give a talk on the conquest of Everest; the death of a friend under a car when the jack collapsed and the car fell on him; one of our servants literally going insane and having to be removed to hospital; the interesting visit of the Oxford University Press representative in South Africa, a liberal South African of Huguenot ancestry with great feeling for the black people there, but who understood the problems of development; the excellent art sessions in some of the African schools, conducted at my request by an art teacher from the European schools, whom I had the honour of giving away at her wedding before we left Chingola; meeting and working with a fine African chief, Ikelenga, a most impressive gentleman; the visit of the world famous golfers, Locke and Thompson; and my involvement with athletics once again, training African boys and seeing them respond to the interest in them.

The final event was perhaps the most surprising: a rather curious offer from the Colonial Office of a post back in Cyprus, phrased in very vague language and giving no assurance that I could not simply go back to continue where I had left off. (By then, the troubles had begun in Cyprus, terrorism was building up, and I suspect they hoped to get back someone who spoke Greek reasonably well and had some understanding of the people there. Needless to say, I did not accept the offer.) We left Chingola, knowing that we would be returning to Africa, to Northern Rhodesia, but we were given no idea of exactly where in the territory. The mighty men in the 'Biscuit Factory' gave little away, and even that always at the last minute! But that did not detract from the enjoyment of our leave, especially our first train journey down to the Cape, crossing part of the Kalahari Desert on the way, and spending several days in Cape Town before we set off on the long sea journey home.

4

The Land of the River

Our time in New Zealand came to an end early in April 1957, and we set off on our way back to Africa, this time on board the 'Southern Cross', which we found quite pleasant with plenty of room to move around, despite the large number of passengers it carried. In May we were in Cape Town, on African soil once more, but still not aware of our final destination in Northern Rhodesia. Just before we left on the train, heading for Bulawayo and Lusaka, I got word that I had been posted to Mongu in Barotseland, an area astride the Zambesi to the west of the territory, bordering on Angola, and one of the most remote parts of the country. We set off, wondering just what lay ahead for us in a place nearly four hundred miles from the railway line, cut off for part of the year by the annual flooding, except by light aircraft. It sounded as if we might meet problems and yet it opened up the prospect of a different kind of life for us in what were the real back-blocks of Africa. We shrugged and smiled, perhaps a little ruefully, as we moved north again up the Karroo and across the Kalahari towards the plateau and the rain forest. We both felt as if the country beckoned; the spell of Africa was already beginning to take hold after only three years.

Barotseland, the land of the river, the land of the Lozi people, was unique within Northern Rhodesia. It was a protectorate within a protectorate. Northern Rhodesia had come under British rule as a protectorate destined for independence, although the time-scale in which this independence was to be achieved was not determined for a long time. Barotseland was a kingdom in itself that was peacefully persuaded to come under British protection: largely, and rather strangely, on the advice of the Paris Evangelical Mission, a French Protestant mission that had operated in the area since 1884. In 1897 the first resident representative of the British South Africa Company, the recognised agent of the British Crown, arrived in Lealui, the capital of Barotseland's paramount chief, then Lewanika. The concession agreement was signed in 1900, giving the Company mineral and trading rights, except in certain reserved areas, as well as administrative and judicial rights over white people there. In return, the Company agreed to protect the territory from outside interference and to assist in education and communication matters. The entry of white men was to be restricted, the paramount chief being able to reserve whatever parts of his kingdom he chose for the exclusive use of his own people. He was also to receive an annual subsidy. In 1906 the chief abolished slavery in Barotseland, and soon afterwards the custom of demanding twelve days' unpaid labour from each of his subjects. The new administration compensated him for the loss of this service from his people. The old custom of tribute to the chief also disappeared. The administration collected a hut tax, a percentage of which was paid back to the chief, and the rest of which went into a fund for the benefit of the people. The agreements reached between Lewanika and the British South Africa Company were the basis for the relationship between Barotseland and the British Crown, and they still stood at the time of independence in 1964. The relationship was never one of master and servant, but a relationship of equals, something that was always carefully observed. Even in my time this was still the case. Government officers who wanted to see the paramount chief for any reason had to make a formal request for an audience through the *ngambela*, the equivalent of a prime minister in Barotseland. There was also a well-established protocol to be observed in conferring with the paramount chief. I am led to believe that much of this has been whittled away in the years since independence and Barotseland has now lost some of its distinctive character.

The Lozi people regarded themselves as superior to the rest of Northern Rhodesia and probably still do. They stated proudly for many years that the main export of Barotseland was brains and, when one looked at what Lozi people had achieved elsewhere and the power they often wielded, it seemed much more than an idle tribal boast. The records which exist show that the Lozi, who in their early stages were known as the Aluyi, appeared in the area some time in the seventeenth century, either from the Congo Basin or from Angola or, most likely, from both. They were fierce, warlike people, gradually spreading south, conquering other tribes as they went. By the beginning of the nineteenth century they had made themselves masters of the Zambesi plains, but inevitably they also fought among themselves; the records tell of invasions, rebellions and civil war spread over many years. In the 1820s, however, a new element arrived on the scene; the Makololo, led by a powerful chief, Sebituane, drove northward from Basutoland, now Lesotho, following the river and subduing in turn the Batoka, the Baila, and finally the Lozi. (It is interesting to note that Livingstone met Sebituane in 1851; he liked and trusted him and the feeling seems to have been mutual.)

The Lozi, driven back to the north by the Makololo and held there for many years, never gave up their struggle to take back the rich Zambesi plains. In 1864, with Sebituane now dead and a period of confusion prevailing, the Lozi swept south, defeated the Makololo, and again became masters of the plains. Thereafter, despite periodic upheavals, they remained, and the Zambesi plains became the centre of Barotseland, as is the case to this day. The present Lozi royal family began its rule in 1878 with another Lewanika, who, despite being driven out once in 1884, came back in 1885 to win a final victory. From then onwards the paramount chief was never really challenged again and Lewanika, in spite of being the 'man of blood' he said he was, gradually settled his people to a life of peace and stability.

Barotseland has quite a well-documented history for over a hundred years, largely thanks to the missionaries and to the pride of the Lozi people themselves, who have always wanted their lifestyle and their achievements to be known, not only to their own people, but also beyond their country's boundaries. Barotseland is, of course, dominated by the Zambesi river, and for centuries the people living there have depended on it to supply them with water, and on its silt deposits to fertilise the plains during the dry season. The provincial boundaries laid down in the early days of

European involvement carefully followed the far older limits of the African kingdom. Barotseland, in fact, covers an area about the size of Ireland, or slightly larger than that of the North Island of New Zealand. Much of this area is plains land, in the wet season almost entirely flooded to varying depths, producing a sheet of water something like eighty miles long and up to fifty miles wide. In the remote past the flood area was even greater, for almost every corner of Barotseland has a covering of sand, making the areas that no longer flood regularly difficult to cultivate without irrigation. Many villages have two sites: one out on the plain near the main stream of the river for the dry season, and another in the surrounding hills for the wet season. The inhabitants move back and forth each year as the flood rises and falls. It is an ancient tradition that no one moves until the paramount chief moves from his plains capital, Lealui, in his hill capital, Limulunga. As the flood is not always consistently the same depth, sometimes villagers are wading around their plains village for days, their huts standing in water, until the chief makes his ceremonial move away from the plain. However, the people never complain and would never think of moving off on their own.

One of the striking features of the annual flood is the fairly rapid rise of its level and the vast, glittering sheet of water that results, followed by the gradual change to a great sea of green, dotted with patches of shining water, as the grass grows up through the water to the surface, creating in many places the illusion of a smooth, grassy plain. In the wet season boats and canoes ply across the flood, but paddles must always be carried as weeds and grass can very quickly choke an outboard engine. Whatever else may have changed in the land of the Lozi, the flood will not change, unless a new dam is built which would probably mean creating a lake out of the Barotse plains. In the dry season the plain produces crops round every village and provides grazing for cattle over a wide area. In our days there, if you wanted fresh milk, you employed a milk boy, a teenage African, whose job was to go out from the Mongu hill each day on to the plain, locate the milking herds, buy the milk and return. This entailed miles of walking, the milk kept reasonably cool and fresh by wrapping it in wet cloths. At home we operated a hand separator, the milk and cream being organised when the milk boy got back, the time of this varying, of course, according to how far he had to go to find the herds. The herdsmen stayed with their herds night and day; it did not rain at all at that time of the year and they lit large fires at night to protect the herds and keep themselves warm. Fuel was a constant problem, but somehow they always seemed to find it. The dry plain provided little cover, so lions and hyenas tended to live and hunt on the edges of it, near the hills and the bushland. A herd far out on the plain was comparatively safe.

Life in the villages was very much subsistence living. Growing crops was not easy, but every stream was utilised and I saw some intricate and well-developed irrigation systems in some very remote and unlikely places. Maize grew well on the plains, but in the remote western areas cassava was a major food crop. This has low nutritional value, but grows well in the poor, sandy soil. It was always rather surprising to see Lozi villagers as fit and healthy as they were, but living in these conditions for a long time had helped them to adapt and make the most of their surroundings. The plain had virtually no trees; perhaps one or two in each village. There was, however, a very tall, prominent palm in one village that stood out for miles across the flat country. Somehow it resisted the flood year after year, sticking up out of the water in defiant isolation each wet season. It had been there for many years when I first saw it, and for all I know may even still be standing there now. The river banks were heavily dotted with gardens in the dry season, which never really disappeared from view totally despite flood waters year after year. A few villages, built on knolls, stayed above water all year round, but when the flood spread out around them, there was little room for gardens to keep them in food. Those near the edges of the plain could communicate and supply themselves by canoe, keeping their villages alive all year round, but the great majority of the plains dwellers had to move each year.

Further back from the river, the land rose to low, rolling hills with very sandy soil and a fuller covering of trees and scrub as one moved further away from the plain. Throughout Northern Rhodesia the trees are comparatively short, averaging perhaps twenty to thirty feet, and they have a distinctive flat-topped appearance, as if some giant had been along to clip them all neatly like some vast hedge. None of this country could be called jungle; it is bushland with the ground beneath the trees comparatively sparsely covered. One could often stand under the trees and look across the top of the scrub for hundreds of yards. In the higher country wildlife was abundant, but the noise of a vehicle usually drove it into hiding. In the settlements the major wildlife problems came from snakes and ants, the latter being particularly persistent and ferocious. Out in the bush one had to be especially watchful for hyenas, which have an incredibly powerful bite. I once helped to get an African villager to a mission hospital who had more than half his foot bitten clean off in a single bite as he slept just inside the doorway of a hut. On my tours I very rarely camped out in a tent, but usually slept in the back of my Land-Rover if I was not in a school building or a rest house or a mission. I still remember being awakened once in the middle of the night by heavy bumping against my Land-Rover. With frightening visions of an elephant standing over my vehicle, I very cautiously peered out through the tough, laced-up, canvas canopy. In the bright moonlight I could see two large hyenas scratching about around my fire and underneath the vehicle. I shone my torch on them, and with ill-tempered, frustrated snarls they paused for a moment to stare at the light before making off at high speed into the bush.

The roads of Barotseland were, in fact, tracks. The sand and the amount of traffic made any fully formed road impractical. In the dry season on the hills, vehicles ground through the sand; in many places villagers had contracts with the public works department to cut grass and lay it across the vehicle tracks on the roadway, helping to give wheels much more grip. On the flood plain the ground became quite hard and driving was normally possible – allowing for the holes and the bumps! Tributaries of the river could usually be forded, but the Zambesi itself had to be crossed by a pontoon ferry, usually paddled by long, broad-bladed oars. It took about half an hour to get across with the current, but returning, against the current, could sometimes take a couple of hours. The chief trouble with the ferries was that they were distinctly erratic in their operation. If things were quiet on the road, the ferry crew often dispersed to the nearest villages, to which they belonged, leaving one man behind on watch. When a vehicle arrived, the driver first had to wake up the watchman, almost invariably asleep, who then went off to round up the crew, an operation that could take an hour or even longer. One did not count time by normal Western standards out in this area. However, the ferrymen always seemed to be a cheerful group and just about every crew I encountered sang as they paddled the heavy pontoon slowly on its way. They were also always very interested in where you had been and where you were going; sometimes quite heated arguments developed among them as to your best route to your destination, but things always finished up with laughter and more singing. I suppose those ferries still operate now as they did thirty years ago – and probably just as erratically and cheerfully.

Most African houses in the villages were rondavels, the round huts with conical roofs seen throughout much of Africa. Among the Lozi the thatching was remarkably good and lasted for a long time in the areas that did not get the annual flood. I was intrigued by the skill of the village thatchers and by the fine finish of their work and did some quiet research as I went round on my tours. From villagers and missionaries, I discovered that quite a long way back, before the turn of the century, one mission had brought out on its staff two expert thatchers from Essex. These men had taught their craft to other Europeans and to many Africans, and the skill spread rapidly, but because Barotseland was so remote and isolated, it did not go beyond the Lozi people. Nowhere else in Northern Rhodesia did I see such fine thatching and such pride in the work. It was not only the small rondavels that were well thatched; large buildings like schools were equally well roofed. In the settlements, like Mongu, all the housing, African and European, was thatched. Our house in Mongu was re-thatched while we were there, and ten years' accumulation of birds, bats and insects was removed, although the metal ant course in the walls had at least kept out the ants.

Many villages made themselves into enclosures by linking the outer huts with fences of wood and reeds, woven together as was done for the doors of the huts. The doors were not hinged, but lifted into slots; they were light and could be lifted away quite easily. The fencing was more permanent and usually about six feet high, the main purpose being to keep out scavenging hyenas and, if the village happened to be near the river or a tributary, the occasional crocodile wandering in the night. The hyena and the crocodile rank among the most disliked creatures, though probably the most dangerous is the buffalo, which will hunt the hunter if he is not very careful. The hyena is very much a scavenger, eating what is left by lions or leopards, often once it is well advanced in decomposition and very malodorous. It is also a very ill-tempered animal, even with its own kind. It does hunt, of course, but seems to prefer someone else to do the hunting for it. The villages that were fenced in closed up their fencing as it got dark, opening up again as soon as it began to get light. Most such villages were small, maybe only a dozen huts or so. The nocturnal predators usually kept clear of larger settlements, which normally had fires burning all night.

For the touring government officers – and there were many of us in administration, forestry, water development, health and education – the land of the Lozi was well supplied with rest houses: quite sizeable thatched huts built of sun-dried bricks, floored, and with mosquito nets over the beds or screens on the doors and windows. In those days there was no trouble with vandalism. The rest houses were checked regularly by the public works department and were always found in reasonably good repair. In most places, of course, there was no electricity, and in the remoter spots there was just a large hut and nothing else, so the touring officer had to supply himself with whatever he needed: pressure lamps; food; drink, hard or otherwise; bedding. His driver and his messenger, if he had one with him, normally slept in the nearby village. Africans usually respected one's privacy and did not lurk round the rest house. On one occasion, however, I visited a very remote school, right off the beaten track; no European education officer had been there before, so as long as daylight lasted I found myself surrounded – at a respectful distance – by numerous young children. I found out from the headmaster that these children had in fact never seen a white man before, since the last European to visit the spot had been an administrative officer some seven years before. It felt quite a curious sensation to be the first white man these children of five and six had ever seen.

Mongu itself was the nearest to what might be called a town in Barotseland. It was, in fact, just a large village with a small commercial area, the government offices, and a European residential area added to it. It had a hospital with a small, well-qualified nursing staff and two or three doctors, who had to tour around the whole area as well as look after the hospital. Mongu sits on quite a prominent hill, overlooking the plain. On clear days one can see for miles and pick out the villages dotted here and there, especially in the dry season, when they are all occupied. A few miles to the north-west lies Lealui, the traditional dry season capital of the paramount chief, much older than Mongu, but not looking its age as many of its buildings are rebuilt each year when the flood subsides. The chief's wet season capital, Limulunga, is out to the north-east, a little further away, on the high ground among the trees and the scrub, so it is not easily seen at all. The northern end of the Mongu hill drops steeply down to the edge of the plain. There is a canal linking Mongu with the river even in the dry season, but when the flood is at its height the township looks out over what appears to be almost an inland sea.

On the point of the hill stands the Residency, the equivalent in other provinces of the provincial commissioner's house, but here he was called the Resident Commissioner. The house was a rambling, impressive place with pleasantly secluded gardens and a fine outlook on to the plain. Like everyone else, the resident commissioner had to get good soil brought up from the plain to keep his garden growing, as the natural soil was extremely poor and sandy. Next to the Residency lay the cluster of government offices, including those of the African education department and, shortly after we arrived there, the small European school. The hill sloped gently to the south, with a road on the ridge and another lower down on the eastern side. Between the government offices and the commercial area down the hill were most of the European houses, all with a good view over the plain. On the edge of the plain was a permanent stream where many European residents, including ourselves, kept small garden plots to grow vegetables. By digging trenches on the hill, and carrying good soil up by Land-Rover to fill them, most of us maintained flower gardens around our houses, but it did not make for easy gardening.

There were trees on the hill, a few round each house, and also a forest nursery, so there was always fuel for fires. The bath water was heated outside in a big boiler and carried inside in buckets as required. Most houses had one open fireplace; sometimes in the evening it was cold enough in the dry season for a fire to be needed. The kitchen had a wood stove. Up on the hill to the western side there were also the remains of an old airstrip, disused by the time we were there, as it was too short by then even for the small planes that flew in to Mongu. There was a much larger and better airfield on the other side of the settlement. The old one was widely used for golf, for flying kites, and for kicking a football, as well as for walks in the evening.

Ants were quite a problem all over Barotseland, especially in the wet season, when the flood drove them up off the plain to the higher land. The ants moved in a column, straight over or through everything in their path, eating completely anything they could, which often meant that sleeping hens were attacked and killed. We were always very careful about keeping ants out of the house, especially away from where the children slept. Frixos, our cat, was never troubled; he quickly got rid of any that he found on him. There were plenty of insects, including mosquitoes, but our houses were wired and we used mosquito nets out in the bush. Snakes were an ever-present danger, although many of them were not, in fact, poisonous. Unfortunately few people, even among the Africans, really knew enough about the snakes to be able to tell which were dangerous and which were not, so snakes in the vicinity of property were quickly chased off or killed. Bats abounded and liked thatched roofs, under which they often lived. Many houses had fine wire netting inside the roof to keep the bats out, but they still got in from time to time. I sometimes found their droppings on the dining table, and occasionally one would land on my head as I sat reading or listening to the radio!

The Lozi people are deeply traditional and, being remote from the general surge of modern life, have managed to preserve their pride and their dignity. I cannot see that changing much, though I believe there have been inroads into the Barotse way of life since independence. In the 1950s the Lozi possessed a calm dignity, good manners and politeness that never made them subservient.

As servants they were respectful and generally quiet, but one never thought of them as menial. Their teachers were the same, and I dealt with hundreds of them in my time there. They gave the impression that they felt themselves to be people just as good as any Europeans, and yet this pride never descended into arrogance. Where they knew that Europeans had superior knowledge and experience, they respected that and wanted to learn from it. Where they knew that they had superior knowledge and experience – such as in understanding the bush and the river and their way of life – they expected respect from the European in return. No important steps were taken, especially in Barotseland, without consulting headmen and chiefs and, if it were necessary, the paramount chief himself. It was traditional for the ordinary village people, when a person of any importance passed, to crouch by the wayside and clap their hands, something they could always manage to do without the least loss of dignity. As an education officer travelling around the area, I frequently met with this response and I always made a point of slowing down my vehicle and leaning out to call a word or two as I passed. I learned that this was much appreciated, for many officers would unthinkingly shoot past in a cloud of dust with little recognition evident.

African servants everywhere were interesting people, but perhaps especially so among the Lozi. To work in a European household conferred a certain prestige and was a job generally desired and highly regarded among Africans. The idea that servants were some sort of slaves made the Africans themselves laugh, let alone us. They had a high regard for children, especially for boys because of the traditional attitude to women in their society. We used to laugh to ourselves in more than one place we were stationed on noticing that even the ironing was carefully graded: mine always came first, followed by our small son's, then my wife's, and finally our daughter's. However, one never commented on this. It was all part of their customs and tradition. They were always fiercely protective of the children and in Mongu we could leave our children asleep at night to go out to a function, safe in the knowledge that the servant on duty in the house would not let us down. The lengths to which this was carried were brought home to us very forcibly just after we had arrived in Mongu and had to go out to a dinner party. Our cook was staying in the house. On our return we came into the house to find the cook on a chair just outside the children's bedroom door, sitting propped against the wall with a carving knife across his knees! When we appeared on the scene in the dim lamplight, he was on his feet in an instant, the knife held out towards us; it was lowered only when I called his name and he could see who we were.

It was interesting and puzzling to find that our cook in particular could always tell us where our children were if they were out of the house. Brennian often went for long walks round the township with his friend, Jeremy, the son of the district commissioner; walks that took them through the African village and down to the edge of the plain. The cook, John, could always tell us where they had been and where they were heading; if necessary, we could have gone out and found them in a vehicle in a matter of minutes. It seemed to be a sort of bush telegraph in operation and was amazingly efficient and accurate. The two small boys learned a lot about Africans and how they lived on these walks, acquiring a natural approach to Africans, an approach that seemed to get over the difference in the colour of the skin. We were well aware, however, that in a town, especially one on the railway line, this easy mingling would not have been possible. The superficial sophistication of town life stole from the African his quiet and dignified approach. Town children were all too frequently loud and cheeky, just like many white children back in their own countries, especially in the poorer city areas. In the country areas of Northern Rhodesia black children were always fascinated by white children; they would follow them round, watching what they did, talking quietly among themselves, but not approaching too close. Our children learnt to treat black Africans just as they treated other whites, without any awkwardness because of colour, and that relaxed attitude seems to have stayed with them to this day.

My work in Barotseland was distinctly different from that I had experienced in the Western Province districts of Ndola and Chingola. From our headquarters in Mongu, we looked out on a vast territory with no real towns, no formed roads, no private cars, no electricity for the earlier part of our time there, miles of flood water for part of the year and a land of one people (although there were various sub-tribes in different areas). The schools were comparatively small, many of them mission schools, and there were numerous missions operating in the area, the largest being the Paris Evangelical Mission and the Capuchin Fathers. Many of the Paris Mission personnel were, in fact, Swiss, while the Capuchin Fathers were all Irish. Though poles apart on many aspects of religion, these two bodies of missionaries got along remarkably well together, thanks largely to good leadership and a sensible tolerance on both sides.

There were some large schools at the main mission centres, particularly at the Paris Mission at Sefula, about ten miles from Mongu, and at the big Capuchin centre at Lukulu, about ninety miles up the Zambesi to the north. Most of these larger mission stations also operated hospitals. Without the missions, many remote areas would have had much less in the way of elementary education and health care. One rather surprising mission was run by the Seventh Day Adventists at the river crossing at Sitoti, some eighty miles south of Mongu. It was run by an American couple – he a qualified teacher, she a qualified nurse – and they managed to keep a good school and a hospital going. I considered them to be two of the most dedicated missionaries I encountered. They were very strict with themselves and their flock – they naturally had a church there as well – but also friendly and hospitable. Their strictness about 'stimulants' caused them to drink only water, fruit drinks, or tea made from lemon leaves. Some officers would never call in at Sitoti because the atmosphere seemed to embarrass them, but many of us always made a special point of stopping there, even if only for half an hour; we knew how lonely those people must have got at times.

Our first year among the Lozi, a year that did not actually start until May, was spent getting ourselves organised and settling in. There was more to this than at first met the eye. We had to get accustomed to pressure lamps, oil lamps, and candles, as well as a wood stove in the kitchen. The ordinary electric torch became a vital piece of equipment. There was also the matter of a kerosene-burning refrigerator – it never ceased to intrigue me that one kept a kerosene lamp burning all the time in order to keep things cold! This refrigerator was very efficient but had just one snag. Now and again, in a draught or if a wick needed trimming, it smoked, sending up a soot-laden column from the back of the fridge and putting a fine black deposit over everything. I quickly learned that the African servants, with the exception of the cook, were not very good with the refrigerator or the pressure lamps. The main problem with the pressure lamps was that they had a mantle similar to the old-fashioned gaslight mantle of the early 1900s and a jolt could break it. Moreover, the pressure lamps could smoke like the refrigerator, with a similar result. It quickly became accepted that only the cook or I ever touched the lamps or the refrigerator. In a matter of weeks I found myself quite an expert, and the cook and I often had profound discussions on methods of filling, pumping, and regulating the lamps.

We had a household of five servants: the cook, who at over fifty was old for an African; the house boy; the kitchen boy; the garden boy; and the milk boy. Apart from the cook, they were all literally boys, teenagers who had left school at Standard IV, so he had no trouble ruling them with a firm hand. Each one knew his job and generally kept strictly to his own domain. Any encroachment led to a rather noisy altercation; any lapse led to an equally noisy ticking off from the cook. But in general, despite occasional changes of personnel in the time we were there, they were a happy lot and we grew to understand one another pretty well. In the house and garden my wife was director of operations and, whatever the African attitude to women might be, all the servants recognised this; especially, of course, as she was on the spot for much of the time and could check up on them, even when she was away teaching for part of the day.

For about two years the European community had been trying to get a primary school in Mongu. There were some twenty children of school age from government and commercial homes, but the problem had been finding a teacher. Now Hazel had arrived – trained, experienced, and already registered in Northern Rhodesia. The District Commissioner quickly moved into action and set wheels in motion at the centre for European education in Salisbury in Southern Rhodesia (now Harare in Zimbabwe). We were rather surprised when word came through that no less than the Director of European Education himself was coming to

Mongu to see the situation in person. He duly arrived towards the end of July and proved to be a pleasant and helpful man. Although he could not categorically say so at that stage, it was obvious that he was fully in favour of a school. He stayed three days in Mongu, looking at everything relevant to the establishment of a European primary school and leaving with the promise of action and an early decision. Unusually for government, there actually was rapid action, and within a month word had come through to proceed. The building already earmarked for the new school was rapidly finished, and equipment began to arrive in the early part of September. The school was able to open in the second week of September, with twenty-six children enrolled and with Hazel as teacher. It proved a great success, for it was very much needed by the community. It also proved valuable in drawing the European community closer together through the Parent-Teacher Association that was immediately formed. The children themselves were delighted and a good many mothers were very relieved. There was an official opening of the school at the end of the month, an occasion which I unfortunately had to miss because I was away on an inspection tour in the bush. Apart from being an interested parent, I had no official connection with the European school, since African education was, as I have already explained, a completely separate department.

By the end of 1957 we were well established in Mongu and in its community, kept very busy both at work and socially. The Mongu Club was one of the main European social centres, to which everyone went fairly regularly in their free hours. After nineteen years I began to play tennis again, something I continued to do for the next ten years and more, finishing up a better player than I had ever been when I was much younger. But all that was only a small part of my life. I was now out on tour for anything from fourteen to twenty-one days each month when the schools were open, a fairly strenuous programme, but a very interesting one. I usually travelled with my driver and my messenger. Sometimes our new, young education officer came out with me. At others I was accompanied by a young district assistant or district officer from the administration. In a country like Barotseland different departments often shared their vehicles with others, regardless of whether they were fellow government officers or mission personnel, European or African. There was a friendly spirit there that was not nearly so evident in other provinces.

Before the end of the year, very soon after the opening of the European school, we had what can only be described as a visitation from a team of British members of parliament. Officially they were on a 'fact-finding tour', for there was already controversy and dispute over the federation of Rhodesia and Nyasaland. This particular visit was notable for an attack of food poisoning we all suffered, including our visitors, after lunch at the Resident Commissioner's house. We awoke the following day to violent sickness, my wife actually passing out and falling on the hard floor. Fortunately it passed quickly, and within an hour or two we were pretty well back to normal, although Hazel had a few bruises to show for her fall. The visit of the MPs was regarded as successful, but we realised even then that moves were afoot, both in Africa and in the U.K., to break up the Federation, which did not suit the aspirations of the rising African nationalists nor Britain's image in the United Nations. Socially we found the MPs a fairly pleasant lot, but they all betrayed their almost complete lack of understanding of Africa and its complex problems. They could not see beyond the viewpoint that the only difference between Europeans and Africans was the colour of their skin. Many aspects, of course, they did not wish to see, and they quickly changed the conversation when these came up. It was interesting to meet people whose only real interest in Africa was political and to see how the situation in Africa might be turned to party ends back in Britain.

Touring was quite a strenuous business on roads which were more or less tracks. These could vary from day to day and a lot of driving, especially in the dry season, had to be done in four-wheel drive to cope with the loose, sandy ground. The traveller also got jolted and tossed around a great deal, for all the routes were full of unpredictable holes; a herd of elephants crossing a road can churn its surface into a remarkable state! On at least one or two occasions my driver and I had to get out with a spade to level out some of the worst holes before we could drive on past an elephant crossing. On another occasion we climbed out rather resignedly, when my driver suddenly let out a short, sharp, expressive 'Ah!' and pointed. Right beside where the vehicle stood was a pile of elephant dung, still steaming. We looked round cautiously into the trees and scrub, but could see nothing, yet elephants must have been there, close by, no doubt quietly swinging their trunks and watching, or at least scenting, us. We climbed back into the Land-Rover and ground slowly on over the ravaged road.

Elephants were not very common in the sandy areas of Barotseland, but the countryside abounded in small buck, hyenas, leopards, lions, monkeys and an incredible number of birds. The river was full of crocodiles, hippos, water snakes, and masses of fish, particularly tiger fish and bream, the latter of which made very good eating. Thousands of birds lived along and in the river banks: fish eagles, marabou storks, flamingoes, weaver birds, and innumerable bee-eaters with their distinctive carmine necks. The bee-eaters appeared in thousands, especially in the dry season, nesting in holes dug into the steep river banks while the water level was low. The weaver birds always fascinated us with their carefully constructed, closely woven nests, suspended from high branches to be out of the reach of predators. The fish eagles were the kings of the bird world, it seemed, and their swoops on fish in the river were a joy to behold; they treated humans with lofty disdain, but never let anyone get too close to them. The most common wildlife one saw, apart from the birds, were monkeys, usually the smaller species. Baboons were around in considerable numbers, but usually made off into the bush at the sound of a vehicle. The smaller monkeys would sit up in the trees, screeching and often making distinctly rude gestures; sometimes they pelted vehicles with bits of wood as they drove past below them. But most African wildlife long ago learnt the value of stillness, and many times one would neither hear nor see anything, yet know that they were there.

Along the river the most unpleasant creature was probably the crocodile. These could often be seen sunning themselves on a sandbank, from which they would slide smoothly into the water as soon as they became aware of our presence, even though we might be fifty yards away in a boat or on the river bank. Other animals, even the domestic cattle, chose their drinking places carefully, for a crocodile knocks its prey off its feet into the water with its massive tail and then holds the victim under the water to drown. A crocodile is thoroughly nasty. The hippo, on the other hand, is a generally peaceful, friendly creature with a sense of humour. It will happily swim under a canoe, rise under it to tip it over, and then swim off, snorting in a way that sounds very like chortling laughter. Occasionally hippos get angry and attack, but this is rare. In the evenings they wallow in shallow water, making the most incredible noises of puffing, blowing, and snorting. They often come ashore at night, making their ponderous way about, usually through the middle of a village garden. The Africans abuse them, shrug at them, and laugh, but I never saw an African try to kill a hippo. No doubt they sometimes did, and no doubt there were hippo poachers somewhere in Northern Rhodesia, but those who lived close to the river seemed to have a deep appreciation of the wildlife it supported.

My touring around the schools in the area could take me about 180 miles south, 100 miles north, 140 miles east, and 80 miles west, of Mongu. These were the main routes, but a normal inspection tour took me many miles off into the bush over no actual road at all. It was tiring travel, but never dull. People were always glad to see you, and you to see them, both European and African. The river alongside which I often travelled for many miles, or on which I sometimes travelled by barge, was an endless source of fascination in any season with its waterfalls, rapids, small islands, sandbanks, and its ferries and their cheerful crews. The schools themselves, many of them run by only two or three teachers, were usually long, low-roofed buildings of the customary sun-dried bricks, the sides open from about two or three feet upwards, the roof thatched and with a fairly long overhang to protect the walls from the rain. At first it always seemed quite dark inside after the glare of the sun outside, but my eyes soon adjusted and I realised that the light was really soft and cool and pleasant. Many of the smaller schools still used slates, with exercise books kept only for a few more permanent notes or projects. There were few textbooks and these were kept under strict control by the teachers, who issued them only for the period of use in class. Large blackboards and easels were used, mainly because there was no wall on which to fix a more permanent wall board. Every classroom had a large cupboard, usually with its legs in tins of kerosene or water to keep out the ants. The floor was often just hard-beaten earth. Sometimes the head teacher had a very small area walled round as an office, but, since he also taught a class full time, his classroom usually doubled as his office. The teachers had houses, usually rondavels, occasionally rectangular and larger, on the school grounds, which generally bordered on a small village. The children came from any villages within walking distance, which might might be as much as eight or ten miles away.

The teaching naturally varied a great deal, much depending on the ability of the head teacher and, in the case of many mission schools, the interest shown by the mission personnel themselves. As a rule, the larger the controlling mission, the better the standard in the schools, mainly because they were sufficient people available to go round the schools regularly. Local education authority schools were visited regularly by the local manager of schools, who looked after all matters of supply and maintenance. Only an education officer could inspect schools, but many managers kept teachers up to the mark with a bit of unofficial inspection and by a quiet word to the education officer from time to time. The main task of the education officers was to instil into the teachers the sense of what was right and good in teaching and the need to keep up standards to a high level. In the early stages, especially, this was not always easy, for some teachers in the lower classes of the primary schools had not, in fact, gone right through secondary school themselves. As time went on, it was possible to raise the level of qualification for entry to teacher training and so the standard of teaching gradually rose. As that standard rose, it became possible to demand higher standards in inspection, creating a virtual spiral of improvement in the educational process.

Inspection often had its humorous side. I once arrived at a remote two-teacher school about mid-morning to find one very young junior teacher desperately coping with two full classes by rushing from room to room, spending a few minutes with each class in turn. There was some panic when I appeared on the scene and asked where the head teacher was. The desperate young man, whose English was not very good in a remote spot like this, stared at me for some time, his eyes shooting across towards the teachers' houses every few seconds. Eventually he blurted out, 'In bed!' 'Is he sick?' I asked. There was another long, uneasy pause before his answer. 'No, sir. But his wife need him!' I managed to keep a straight face and sent him off to the head teacher's house to tell that gentleman he had five minutes to get across to the school block to his class. There was dead silence, while every child in the school watched the progress of the junior teacher across to the houses. About three minutes after he disappeared into the head teacher's house, the head teacher emerged at the double, fastening his belt and beating his junior back to me by a short head. 'Are you alright?' I asked him, 'Ready to take your class over?' He looked at me with wide eyes. 'Yes, bwana, yes.' He then added, with deadly seriousness, 'But my wife very sick!' Again I kept a straight face and refrained from asking him exactly what he meant by that. We all went to work and the inspection went ahead.

On another occasion I arrived at a school shortly before midday and, while talking to the head teacher, I noticed that the clock on his desk was covered with dust and had obviously not worked for some time. Neither teacher had a watch – very few had out in these bush areas – and there was no other clock in the school. I could not resist it. 'Oh, by the way,' I said, 'what's the time?' There was a short, electric pause; then the teacher shot outside and studied the sky and the sun. He came back in. 'It's a quarter to twelve, sir.' He was only about seven minutes out! I solemnly thanked him and suggested he put his clock right, which he did with similar solemnity. Not along afterwards, when the afternoon classes began, we went on with our work. Moreover, he ran a good little school; I contemplated on how things can run smoothly and regularly without our slavish subjection to clocks and time.

The new year of 1958 began with the wettest wet season for many years and, as a result, a record flood across the Zambesi plains. Touring around was always more difficult in the wet season. Some schools became virtually inaccessible. Others took twice as long to reach. The rest houses often leaked. The storms were frequent and violent. Minor streams, 'creeks' as we call them in New Zealand, became raging torrents in a very short time, but often went down just as quickly, so sometimes I just sat in my

Land-Rover and waited, perhaps an hour, until I could safely drive through the water. But the wet season also brought one of the great events of Lozi life: the *kuomboka*.

Kuomboka literally means 'to get away from the water', which is exactly what happened. The paramount chief made a ceremonial progress each year across the flooded plain from Lealui to the hill village of Limulunga, just off the plain, where he had a permanent palace. Lealui, unlike some plains settlements, was not washed away in the flood. It went partially under water, but became uninhabitable for some months. The buildings, or most of them, usually survived to be refurbished for use later when the flood receded. We witnessed the *kuomboka* twice and it was, without doubt, something worth seeing. In 1958 conditions were dull, with rain at intervals, but the next year we had a beautiful day which made for an extremely colourful ceremony. Procedure was always identical for both Europeans and Africans. Government departments, at least the larger ones, had their own barges and paddlers. African education had a big barge: wide, flat-bottomed, half of it covered, half open to the sky. As the *kuomboka* occurred in the warm weather, getting wet did not really matter; in fact, the paddlers revelled in it. We had sixteen paddlers, under the command of our head messenger, Kaputeni, who got his name, I am sure, from the position he held as captain. This was one of his big days in the year and he made the most of it.

Before eight in the morning we all assembled at the landing at the foot of the Mongu hill and boarded the barge, which, amid much shouting, was pushed off into the deeper water. We were on our way. The paddlers soon picked up their rhythm and chanted as we headed out across the plain that had become a great sheet of water. Various barges, government and commercial firms, were all on their way and it was a point of honour, if it could be managed, to reach Lealui first. On this, our first occasion, we were narrowly headed off by Sutherlands, one of the big general stores, to land at Lealui second. The journey took us about two hours; on the way we passed one or two small villages with little more than their thatched roofs showing, the inhabitants having already taken their canoes and belongings over to Lealui to follow the paramount chief as soon as they heard the drums begin to beat early the day before.

We also passed one or two clumps of trees standing up out of the water, festooned with the nests of weaver birds. Much of Lealui itself was still just above water, but houses on the outskirts of the village were awash and the flood was still rising. We all got ashore dry and then had a wait of about half an hour before the paramount chief, Mwanawina III, appeared.

For the occasion, the chief wore a pale coloured frock-coat, a hat, and carried his ceremonial fly-whisk. Ahead of him walked a minor chief, carrying his umbrella, still rolled up, as the rain had fortunately stopped, though the sky was still heavily overcast. Behind him came one of his personal bands, playing as it moved along. The chief had several of these bands, each of five or six men, and on special occasions such as the *kuomboka*, they played in turn almost continuously. On this day they played all day throughout the journey and after arrival at Limulunga. The chief proceeded slowly from his Lealui palace through the village down to the water's edge. The huge royal barge, the *nalikwanda*, was drawn in as far as possible until it began to ground on the slope, but there was still water to be negotiated, so a long shallow canoe was drawn in to bridge the gap. It was held steady by men standing in the water, while the chief stepped into it, walked its length, and was then able to step up into the massive *nalikwanda* perfectly dry. The huge royal drums, the *maoma*, were already on board and, as soon as the chief was safely in the shelter of the high canopy, these began to beat.

The *nalikwanda* is very long and heavy, and is propelled by about forty paddlers. How they managed to move it at all puzzled me, but they did and, once it was fully afloat, the paddlers jumped in. The paddlers are traditionally *indunas*, who are chiefs and members of the chief's council or *kuta*, and lesser chiefs selected for their skill as paddlers. Tradition also has it that in the old days a paddler who missed a beat or did not paddle satisfactorily was tossed into the flood to be taken by the crocodiles. The tossing into the water undoubtedly did take place, but at no stage would any self-respecting crocodile come within half a mile of the great barges and the mass of small canoes as the flotilla moved across the plain towards the hills. So the latter part of the legend is very unlikely to contain much truth. Maybe the

69

crocodiles were bolder and more ferocious a couple of hundred years ago.

The *nalikwanda* leads the movement across the flood and nothing, not even the smallest canoe, must get ahead of it. Close behind comes the barge of the chief's senior wife, the *muoyo*. On the occasions when I saw the *kuomboka*, she was a lady of very ample proportions, who was reputed to weigh twenty-two stone. The distance between Lealui and Limulunga in a straight line is no more than perhaps fifteen or sixteen miles, but the route followed by the barges and canoes zigzagged across the flooded plain, so that the journey took most of the day. Once in the clearer water, with forty paddlers swinging in unison to the beat of the drums, the barges can build up a remarkable speed, leaving many of the canoes well behind them. The canoes, shallow and narrow dug-outs, loaded with possessions and often a whole family, appear lucky to stay afloat at all, but they usually do so and manage to keep near enough to the barges to be able to land fairly close behind them at Limulunga. The royal paddlers all wear a sort of kilt, often a leopard-skin, and a very distinctive lion-skin headdress. Their paddles are as long as oars, but have a broad blade; the paddling is all done standing up.

Once the procession was on its way out across the water, we spectators hurried back to our own barges and headed back for Mongu, a trip of about two hours. Once back there, we piled into our various departmental vehicles and set out on the sandy hill road to grind our way to Limulunga. We reached there in time to see the flotilla approaching; the big drums beating a steady rhythm, the chief's band chiming in, the paddlers also chanting. It was an impressive sound, as well as sight. Awaiting the chief on shore outside his palace and around the landing place were hundreds of Africans, a reception committee of chiefs, and all the senior government officers, headed of course by the resident commissioner. As the chief's barge moved smoothly in to the landing, the drums stopped, the band stopped, the chanting stopped, and the people all around fell quiet. There was then a moment of most impressive silence. After this, singing and cheering broke out all around. The chief came up the bank from the *nalikwanda* to be greeted by the resident commissioner. There

70

followed a solemn progress up the hill to the palace where a chosen few, both European and African, were able to go inside with the chief for some refreshments. His band struck up again as they moved into the palace precinct and passed from our view. A little later, however, the chief appeared on the steps of the palace, accompanied by the resident commissioner in response to calls from the crowd outside.

The crowd around the front of the palace was an interesting and colourful mix of young and old, but it was the older people, especially the women, who showed their feelings most. Small groups sang and danced their way right up to the palace gate and back again. Many larger groups squatted where they could see through the gate, chanting and clapping rhythmically, this time with the men in a majority. The *ngambela*, the prime minister of the Barotse people, also appeared in the palace entrance from time to time, but the focus was always on the paramount chief. The idea of royalty is well established among the Lozi and has been for many years. It is also interesting to note that the organisation of the paramount chief's government, very similar in structure to our own British monarchy, is not a copy of it, but was there before the white man appeared on the scene, despite all the upheavals and invasions and civil wars.

One development in Barotseland, however, that does arise from contact with Europeans is dress, in particular that of the women. This comes largely from the missionary influence. The missionaries, especially the early ones, had the usual Victorian inhibitions about the human body, and one of their first concerns usually seemed to be to cover up the native women. Most women found they liked the distinction of wearing a dress and generally raised little objection to missionary efforts to make them 'decent'. In Barotseland this seemed to take a special turn, and before long multiple skirts, gathered at the back into a distinctive bustle effect, became the female attire for special occasions. The *kuomboka*, being one of the greatest occasions of the year, brought out all the best dresses, which were very colourful indeed. As many Barotse women have prominent posteriors anyway, the bustles were most striking!

The women in Barotseland dance without inhibition, but with great grace and dignity. Years later in Western Samoa I was struck by the similarity of their style of dancing to that of the Polynesian people. Dancing by the men was entirely different, the main style being that of the *makishi* dancers, who can be traced back a long way in Lozi history. They are specially costumed and masked to represent various animals and birds and figures from their mythology. Their dancing is vigorous and often blatantly suggestive, some of their actions bringing loud and rather lewd laughter from the crowd. The *makishi* appear on almost any ceremonial occasion, their dancing following a well-established pattern, in contrast to that of the women, which is more spontaneous and individual. Like Europeans, Africans can enjoy both crude, physical humour and more subtle manifestations of the comic spirit. We saw the *makishi* performing at numerous and varied ceremonies, and found they always responded to the mood of the crowd. If the crowd showed that they wanted a little lewdness, they got it – and you did not need to know the language to understand what was going on. My wife and I had several occasions when we had to think fast and express ourselves carefully in explaining what was happening to our children!

We saw the *kuomboka* again in 1959 on a brilliant, clear day; it was even more striking then. I am told that it has now more or less ceased as a spectacle, but I cannot believe that it will ever disappear completely. That would be like abandoning the ceremonial opening of Parliament or doing away with the Lord Mayor's show in London.

The year 1959 was one of steady work for all of us. I was up and down the large province for days on end every month, but touring was always interesting and different places left different impressions. I never felt disgruntled at having to go off into the bush; yet I was always very glad to get home again and find the family waiting, eager to know what had happened on that particular outing. More than once during the year they had all been able to come out with me. Twice we travelled on the river, which the children naturally found much better than the restrictions of a Land-Rover. Moreover, the slower pace of river travel, especially on the barge, enabled us to see more, for there was no engine noise to frighten off the birds or alert the crocodiles a hundred yards or more away. The department also possessed a small launch, so sometimes we made our journey on that. It was much faster — as long as we did not strike weeds or too many reeds near the river bank.

One trip on which the whole family accompanied me took us by Land-Rover to a place called Nakanyaa, where there was one of the 'unmanned' rest houses. This was just a fairly large, substantial thatched hut, with nothing in it except a table and chairs. Visitors had to take everything they might need with them, so we went well equipped with camp beds, a chilli-bin (to keep food cold), and even fuel for our cooking fire. I think my African driver enjoyed travelling with the whole family for a change as much as I did. For the children this was the real thing, especially after dark when we were lit by the fire outside the door, and candles and lamps inside the hut. At first we could hear voices from the nearby village, but soon these died down until later there were just the noises of the bush: owls hooting, the snarling of hyenas, the coughing grunt of a leopard, and lots of rustlings and squeakings we could not identify. We also attracted more than our share of mosquitoes, but our nets protected us at least to some extent. Once we moved in for the night we dropped our door into its slots, but I think the children were glad we were all together in one big room. We kept one light burning all night, for there is nothing blacker than the inside of an African hut in the middle of the night.

The best trip we had *en famille*, however, was a week-long tour up the Zambesi to Lukulu and back when we took the launch, but had the Land-Rover keeping pace with us by road, such as the road was, and carrying a lot of our supplies. Our 'captain' on the river was our supervisor of trades training in the province and was then — and still is after all these years — a very good friend of ours. He commanded the launch and knew the river fairly well, especially where to camp at night, and we spent two nights camping on the way up, arriving at the Capuchin Fathers' mission late on the third afternoon. I was able to inspect a couple of schools on the way.

We made good time on our first day, arriving at our camping site near a village called Libonda just as the sun was setting. The vehicle with our camping equipment was already there to meet us. Camping out by the river, with the snorting of hippos quite close, was a great experience for the family and there was much

73

excitement in the morning when it was obvious that a crocodile had walked right through our camp during the night. We broke camp early and were soon on our way, watched with casual interest by the hippo, with some indignation by the many birds, and with a crafty sort of suspicion by the crocodiles. We paused in the middle of the day at a spot called Silonga, where I spent part of the afternoon inspecting the two-teacher school while the family fished for bream out on the river. Then we moved on smoothly up the river to Ngulwana, camping near the village and its school. The night this time was much warmer and heavier, bringing out the mosquitoes and numerous other unidentifiable insects, but the fire and our nets kept us as protected as we could expect under the conditions. No one worried unduly about time; we all found ourselves going by the sun rather than by our watches!

Next morning I spent some time at the school, following up the launch later in the Land-Rover to rejoin the family, who had moved steadily along, fishing and photographing and watching life on the river. The rest of the day until late afternoon we all did the same, eventually arriving at Lukulu mission to be welcomed by the Fathers, who had their rest house ready for us. As the next day was a Sunday, we were able to spend it in a much more leisurely manner, swimming by a sand bar in the river, and looking around the mission and its various activities. The mission had both boys' and girls' establishments, the Sisters in the latter being as Irish as the Fathers – and with the same outspokenness and sense of humour! I was not inspecting the Lukulu schools on this occasion, so the following day the family set off in the launch with our trades supervisor back down the river for Mongu, while I headed north and east in the Land-Rover, visiting four schools during the day and ending up miles along the Dongwe, a tributary of the Zambesi, in one of the most remote areas in the province. This boasted a remarkably good rest house, probably so good because not many people came there. It looked down on a very attractive series of rock pools, visible at this time because we were right at the end of the dry season. I had three and a half more days of inspection and pounding rough bush tracks after that as I headed back towards Mongu. This area had plenty of wildlife and I got several photos during stops on the way, mainly of hartebeest, monkeys and buffalo. Camped for the night at a spot called Mayankwa, I was awakened in the small hours by the rumbling of lions, close enough to make me get out of my small tent and into the front of the Land-Rover. The lions moved round me in a semi-circle and then off into the night; next morning I was able to establish that they had come within about three hundred yards of my camp. Moving on from there, I spent a couple of nights with the Capuchin Fathers at Mangango, inspecting the school there and also using it as a base for visiting smaller outlying schools. I eventually got home to Mongu some days after the family, who had enjoyed a good trip back down the river, with birds, hippos and crocodiles for company.

Prior to all this, the provincial education officer had gone on leave to the UK. As second in command in the province, I had been officially appointed as acting P.E.O. In fact, I was now next in line for a permanent appointment as a provincial education officer, but I had to wait for the chess pieces to move, so to speak, before I could be placed on the right square. I had to wait another year and a half before the opening presented itself and the great men in Lusaka remembered that I was out there in the bush. Meanwhile, our time in Barotseland was drawing to a close as another leave rapidly approached, and we began to prepare ourselves for yet another move – and yet another new posting when we came back from our leave.

Many incidents keep coming to mind that I have not mentioned so far, things that merit only passing mention, but still mean a lot to us and to our children. There was the excitement of getting electric power in Mongu in March of 1959 after two years of lamps and candles. There was the remarkable occasion when I woke up at 1 a.m. to hear movements in the kitchen. I crept out to find our kitchen boy busy making our morning tea! He had not looked at any clock, but 'just thought it was time'. There was the rather frightening occasion when the house next door but one to us, thatched like our own, took a direct strike of lighting in the first dry storm of the season and went up in flames in a few minutes. The couple who lived there just had time to grab their baby and their dog and frenziedly push their vehicle away from the front door. That scared everyone in Mongu, but the pre-rains storms, fortunately not very frequent, were always dangerous, because everything was so very dry after months of absolutely no rainfall. I also remember our rat hunt in our outside storehouse, which we suspected had been invaded by rats. I assembled the cat, our small son, the garden boy, and the kitchen boy together, and in we went. Frixos, the cat, however, declined to assist in what he considered an idiotic human activity, and sat washing himself on a tree stump, watching us with a sort of amused contempt. We humans went to work fairly successfully nonetheless, killing forty rats and thoroughly cleaning out the storehouse. When we had finished, Frixos inspected the place and then came over to rub elegantly round my legs. The last event of importance before we went off on leave was a combined birthday and engagement party in January for a young New Zealand nurse and a government officer who hailed from South Africa. We had the party at our house; it was the last social function of that nature we held there before leaving Barotseland. The couple, who now live in Australia, have been our friends since those Mongu days and we still communicate regularly to this day.

We flew out of Mongu in the first week of February 1960, to head home to New Zealand for a winter leave. The children both had a term of school in Dunedin – and experienced snow for the first time in their lives. To us New Zealand was home; to them it was a place we visited from time to time, where they saw grandparents and uncles and aunts and cousins they scarcely knew at that stage. For years their home was Africa. I think we all left a bit of ourselves back there each time we went on leave. A spell emanates from Africa.

5

Back to Civilisation?

W e left New Zealand again in August 1960, and by the
end of September were back in the middle of Africa,
having had a pleasant journey by ship and train, our
children now old enough to participate in things with us, thus
making travel easier for us all and far more enjoyable. One event
with a humorous side to it occurred when we reached Africa
again. We had with us two large tins of New Zealand honey
and had not been told that special permission was needed to take
honey into South Africa and the Rhodesias. When we arrived in
Cape Town, a big Afrikaner customs officer asked me for 'the
papers' for the honey; of course, I had no such papers. Afrikaners
are not generally noted for their sense of humour, but this man
had just that. 'It's prohibited without licence, man', he said and
then grinned, adding, 'but if you give it direct to the guard on the
train – so you have no access, eh? – we let the Rhodesian customs
work it out!' I did just as he said and we duly arrived in Bulawayo
to change over to Rhodesia Railways. A very Rhodesian young
customs officer stared in astonishment. 'Christ!' he said, 'How did
you get that past South African customs?' I told him. He scratched
his head. But he, too, had a touch of humour. 'The bastards!' he
said eventually and grinned at me. 'Take it away, man, I haven't
seen it!' And so we got our precious New Zealand honey with us
into Northern Rhodesia.

This time I knew before we left New Zealand that we were
destined for Broken Hill, (known, since independence, as Kabwe).
To most people this was 'back to civilisation' for us, back from the
remote bush, back to the railway line and the main road, back to

all the normal amenities of a fair-sized town almost anywhere in the world, at least in the Western world. We were not so sure about this definition of civilisation. There was a great deal about Mongu and Barotseland and the Lozi people that was more civilised than anything else we saw in Africa. However, here we were, and there *was* much to be said for sealed roads, a regular railway service, and all the amenities at work and in recreation. The mail arrived pretty regularly. The rubbish was collected. One could get milk delivered. There was variety and choice in the shopping area. And there were schools, for both our children and for Hazel, who had a job waiting for her when we arrived in Broken Hill.

Broken Hill was another town that really owed its existence in the first place to mining. The original name for the area that became the town was Mutwe-wa-Nsovu, 'the Elephant's Head', and there were a few European settlers there even before 1900. Chirupula Stevenson had walked all around the area in 1900. In 1902 lead and zinc ores were discovered and, since they were similar to those at Broken Hill in Australia, the place got the name of Broken Hill. Its modern name, Kabwe, had always been associated with the district; even in our time, the government rest house there was called Kabwe Lodge. And Kabwe is a lot simpler than Mutwe-wa-Nsovu. In 1904 the Rhodesia Broken Hill Development Company was formed and mining operations began. This at once galvanised railway development. By 1906 Broken Hill was the northern railhead, and by 1911 the railway had been pushed on to link up with the Congo system. For many years Broken Hill was the headquarters for Rhodesian Railways; it still remains the railway headquarters for Zambia.

In 1927 Broken Hill had the distinction of a royal visit, when the Prince of Wales, later to become the ill-fated Edward VIII, came there to open the Mulungushi dam and power scheme, one of the first such schemes on the African continent. At first the town depended on mining, but commercial development gathered pace, very slowly at first, but later much more rapidly, especially after World War II. Development of the whole area leapt ahead after 1949, and in 1954 Broken Hill became a full municipality, by which time there were about 6,000 Europeans, 400 Asians and 40,000 Africans living there.

The Central Province, with Broken Hill as its centre, despite the fact that Lusaka is larger and is the national capital, was a natural farming area once some of the land was cleared. The land is just under 4,000 feet above sea level, rolling country, with generally good soil and a rainfall of around thirty-six inches a year. Like all of Northern Rhodesia it has a long dry season, but the rainfall seems rather gentler and more evenly spaced over the wet season. The violent storms of the Copperbelt seem much less frequent. It was not long before land was being steadily cleared and more and more farmer-settlers began to arrive to work it. By the time we lived in Broken Hill in the early 1960s, the Central Province had become the main farming area, leading the country in the production of maize and tobacco. It was also a top area for the growing of vegetables and for extensive cattle farming. During the 1950s there was great development in dairy farming, and also large strides in forestry. Despite the fact that the physical appearance of the countryside, and even of the cleared land, was different, the activities around Broken Hill could not help but remind us of New Zealand. By 1960 the Central Province had 50,000 domestic cattle, more than half of these belonging to African farmers, who in this part of the world turned, at least partially, to European styles and methods of farming, meeting with a lot of success.

The Broken Hill mining area was quite different from the Copperbelt. The ores were lead and zinc, not copper, and, when mining began there were technical problems getting the metals out of the ground. Moreover, the ore deposits were mixed in oxidised form and could not be separated on the spot, which meant high transport costs to carry bulk ore further south for refining. Refining, particularly of lead, was eventually operating on the spot by 1915, some ten years after mining had begun. Zinc refining was not fully operational for another ten years. By 1928 all the problems had been solved and the refining processes were at last in full swing – just in time to face a new problem, a water table at 225 feet below the surface that threatened to cause the cessation of all mining by about 1940. But this problem, too, was solved by drainage shafts and pumps, lowering the water level to 1,000 feet below the surface. By the 1960s, the Broken Hill mining operations were very well established, producing high grade lead

79

and zinc, as well as vanadium and cadmium. Broken Hill, however, did not become a mine-dominated, almost mine-ruled, town like those on the Copperbelt. There were too many other interests at work: industrial, commercial, transport and agricultural. It was, in fact, a town of more varied interests and development than the national capital, Lusaka.

In appearance our new home town was very like Ndola and Chingola, but it was not divided in the same way into government, mine, and commercial areas and communities. No one function really dominated here, so the town developed much as a small, prosperous town in New Zealand would do. By the standards of Northern Rhodesia, it had quite a history, going back the best part of a hundred years as far as Europeans were concerned, but mining operations uncovered the fact that men had been there for untold centuries. Fossil bones and stone implements came to light, and in 1921 the skull of a type of man not known before was unearthed, to become known to the world as *Homo Rhodesiensis*. A plaque recording this discovery used to stand on Broken Hill railway station; whether it is still there now, I do not know.

Like most towns in Northern Rhodesia, and in all that part of Africa, Broken Hill was generally well laid out, with streets well planted with trees for shade. It stood beyond the edge of the rain forest proper, but the land was still largely tree-covered. Large tracts of the Central Province had been cleared for farming, making it all the more necessary to have trees in the streets of the town and round the houses. The two main streets, where most of the shops and offices were situated, were Broadway and Davey Avenue. They met at the western end of the central part of the town, where there was a huge tree, which, if my memory serves me rightly, was a wild fig. It was known locally simply as the Big Tree or sometimes the Slave Tree, for in earlier days it had provided a shady slave market for Arab slave traders, the kind of men whom Livingstone encountered and opposed so vigorously. The Big Tree provided a pleasant resting place in the centre of town, and the Africans one saw snoozing must have been far happier than their forbears a century before under the eyes of their Arab captors who regarded them as little more than animals. It is often forgotten that the main slave traders in Africa were Arabs, and that European slave traders appeared scarcely at all in Central Africa, though they were prominent in West Africa.

Our new home was built of burnt brick with a tiled roof, and had all the normal amenities of a town house in New Zealand or the United Kingdom. We had a sizeable garden with a rambling rose hedge down one side and some healthy banana palms at the back. Our children could now both go to the European primary school. Hazel took up a post at the Jasmine Street primary school on the other side of town in a newly developed area near the hospital, which was quite large and well-equipped, with good staff. The main African suburb of Bwacha lay to the north of the town, astride the main road to the Copperbelt and the Congo. Lusaka was just over eighty miles to the south. The main railway line ran right through the western side of the town, just beyond the end of the two main streets. In many ways it was like being back in a New Zealand country town like Gore or Balclutha or Ashburton.

There were naturally many more Africans than Asians in the town, but the Asian presence was more noticeable, since many shops were owned and operated by Indians. The Africans were different in attitude and manners from the Lozi, and showed little of the latter's striking dignity and courtesy. The Central Province lies mainly in the country of the Tonga–Ila group of tribes, the most numerous in the whole country, but it also spread to some degree into Bemba–Lala country, the second most numerous tribal group. The language most frequently heard around Broken Hill was Cibemba, which I had experienced on the Copperbelt, so at least I had no need to face any further language examinations. Rather like in the Copperbelt towns, I found the African attitude here slightly aggressive and lacking in refinement. It was almost as if the Africans in Broken Hill had some inferiority complex, engendered by the presence of so many South Africans, and exacerbated by the fact that in most larger towns much of the tribal unity and spirit had been lost. Just as we see now in other countries – including New Zealand – the indigenous people (or rather the earlier invaders, if one is to be accurate) deprived of their tribal unity and leadership, tend to try to make up for it by a certain loudness and truculence, born of insecurity. I had seen this in Ndola and Chingola; I now experienced it again in Broken Hill.

I cannot claim that there was any particular unpleasantness on the part of the African there; just a lack of the dignity and refinement we had known along the Zambesi River.

I had come back to Africa this time as the deputy provincial education officer of the Central Province, and had been promised that I would be the P.E.O. while the present incumbent was on leave. He was due to go on leave about a month after my arrival. However, on reaching Broken Hill I found that this was not correct; he was now to go on leave in the following March, so I would remain as deputy for six months instead of only one. I was irritated, but not unduly concerned; after the best part of seven years in Northern Rhodesia I knew what to expect from the Biscuit Factory in Lusaka, which was now uncomfortably close at only eighty miles away. Fortunately I already knew and got along well with the present P.E.O., so there were no real problems. We all plunged ourselves into work – myself, my wife, and our children – and set about adjusting ourselves to another place and another slightly different style of life.

Retirement age in the colonial service was still fifty-five, based on colonial life and work in the 1920s and 1930s, when many officers had to retire for health reasons, or even died, before that age. By the standards of the western world in the 1950s and the 1960s, retirement was expected at the age of sixty or even later, so fifty-five was a difficult age to be left in the air. To be in that position in the middle–forties was in some ways even worse: and this was the position in which I found myself in 1960. We were all very interested, therefore, in the Monckton Commission and the report it was to produce in October of that year. Following that, an education conference for Northern Rhodesia was due to take place in London in December. All sorts of rumours flew around, especially in Lusaka, and everyone waited rather edgily and impatiently for what would emerge from all these deliberations. In general, the most worried officers were those in the provincial administration, who really had no specific training for a particular profession. They were mostly involved in duties of a general administrative type particular to the colonial organisation and not to be found back in the United Kingdom, where the Civil Service was already well established over a long period. At least those of us in the fields of education or agriculture or forestry or any other specialised department had a specific field to go back to. We would not be very welcome, as most of us later discovered, but at least there were jobs for us for which we were well qualified. The P.A. men had nowhere certain to turn. I have more to say on the Monckton Commission and the London Conference in a later section that deals more fully with the Federation, so I will not expand on aspects of those here. It is enough to say that from 1960 onwards there was always some uncertainty, which must have affected the attitude and the work of some of our younger members, even in the field of education: the drive and the dedication were blunted to some degree. Meanwhile, we listened to the rumours and assessed them; we listened to the proposals that emerged and assessed those. We kept one eye on the present and one on the future and, as far as the older officers were concerned, we set out to ensure that, when we left, our African successors would take over as well prepared and confident as we could make them. In general, we had a great measure of success, even though we did not get the time we would have liked to thoroughly do what we were aiming to do.

Although we were now living in a sizeable town on the main route through the territory, the Central Province still presented a variety of country and consequently a variety of conditions when one went out on a tour of inspection. To the west lay the extensive Lukanga swamp country, which dried out sufficiently for part of the year to permit people and vehicles to weave their way through at least part of it, but which in the wet season was impassable for vehicles for the most part. The area round Broken Hill and Lusaka was fairly open, rolling country, the openness increased by the amount of clearance for farming, but by New Zealand or United Kingdom standards there was still a lot of tree and scrub cover. To the north-east and the south-east one fairly quickly ran into more rugged country, covered much more heavily with trees. Down to Feira, which lay at the junction of the Luangwa and the Zambesi Rivers, there was a steep escarpment and a narrow, rather tricky road, especially in the wet weather. The road dropped over a thousand feet to reach Feira, a very isolated spot, although a most attractive one in its river setting. Its nearest neighbour was the Portuguese administrative settlement at Zumbo, a mile or so across the river. On one of my visits to Feira, I was given the use of the district commissioner's launch to go across to Zumbo in order to buy some Portuguese wine. This was a regular thing, though officially frowned upon, but the great men from Lusaka did not often venture down to such an isolated settlement. The man who ran the liquor store on the far river bank was a half-caste African Portuguese, who spoke remarkably good English. He was able to practise it pretty regularly – whenever the district commissioner at Feira had visitors!

North-east of Broken Hill the main road, unsealed after turning east at Kapiri Mposhi, led to Serenje and some very rugged country, more and more heavily covered as one went further north, for from here onwards the road moved into the edge of the tropical rain forest. A little way beyond Serenje, one could turn off directly north and climb up to the Livingstone Memorial by the Lulemala River, the place where Livingstone died in May 1873. It is a wild, remote spot, but has a distinct atmosphere about it; at least it did in the 1960s, when I went there. Back on the main road, not far from Chitambo Mission, the northern route crossed into the Northern Province where my territory ended (although later the Northern Province was to become my territory, so I knew both sides of that provincial border very well). Travelling was easier and faster than it had been in Barotseland, though some roads in the wet season became a sea of mud. However, in the dry season, the hard, bumpy ground enabled much greater speed than was possible in the sandy country as long as one avoided the sudden holes or rocks encountered on the more remote tracks.

On the main north–south road there was a constant flow of traffic, mostly heavy commercial transport and smaller government vehicles like my Land-Rover. Off the main road the flow ceased rather abruptly, but one still met quite a number of vehicles, from fairly heavy mission trucks to the old, dilapidated African or Indian light trucks, usually belching blue smoke and making incredible noises. It was small wonder that in this area we saw far less wildlife than we had seen in Barotseland. In the open country there were more villages and hence more people about. Their attitude varied a great deal. One group would wave and smile and call out a greeting, while another would stop and watch, but acknowledge the vehicle only with a slight wave of the hand. Yet another would stare sullenly and make quite clear that we were not popular with them. In the schools, both in the town and out in the bush, the attitude was generally polite, but rather remote. Once I got behind the initial wariness – promotion and progress depended a great deal on education officers of all grades – I usually found a good healthy interest in the work and the children, with a readiness to talk and to learn; although some left–wing teachers, who saw me as an oppressor, never seemed willing to accept me.

Since this area was substantially Bemba-Lala in tribal affiliation, even though there was considerable tribal mixture in the town and especially the mine, we were in an area very subject to political influence. The Bemba, in particular, seemed very attracted to the ideas and promises that emerged from what became the major political party, the United National Independence Party (UNIP), and gave it strong support from the start. Consequently, I saw more political feeling among the people I had to work with from now on, since the Northern Province, where I spent my final years in Africa, is the heart of the Bemba country. The Bemba probably suffered more from the depredations of the Arab slave traders than most other tribes, and one theory propounded was that this had led to a moral weakening, since over the years all the best young men and women in physique and in character had been repeatedly removed from their homeland and their people, but I was always rather sceptical about this. It was true that, generally speaking, the Bemba seemed to lack energy and determination by comparison with the Lozi. Nevertheless, I found plenty of good dedicated teachers working in the Central Province and the standard of the schools was as good – or sometimes as bad! – as anywhere else I had been. Yet again I found, as I began to move around, that many schools had never been inspected, and very few had been inspected in what I felt to be an adequate manner. I also noticed a lack of practical professional knowledge among many education officers, who were well qualified on paper. Some were not interested in improving that side of their work, although among the African staff there was generally speaking a desire to learn more about how and why certain teaching methods should be used. Naturally many had their eyes on the future, when independence would give them a chance to do the work currently done by European officers. Sadly, many of them were to be disappointed, for with independence came the spread of politics into all walks of life, and one had to belong to the right political party to keep moving ahead in the civil service. Numerous poorly qualified and generally inadequate teachers found their way to high positions of responsibility because they were devoted party members or knew precisely whom to fawn upon.

Meanwhile, our work went on. The P.E.O. and I took turns at getting out beyond the town to make our presence felt in schools in all corners of the area we controlled. We had town schools, of course, in Lusaka itself, and I was now able to visit Lusaka without necessarily going to the department headquarters, which I am afraid I always found rather depressing. I always got the impression that people there were so bound up with rules and regulations that they had lost sight of education. I preferred to be out in the bush doing what I could to help the smaller schools, though in this part of the country schools were generally bigger than in Barotseland. I found, however, that buildings were often surprisingly poor, and that villagers and staff did not take the same pride in the appearance of their schools. The standard of work in general, though, was little different. By Christmas 1960, I had managed to see a good deal of the province, but I had not yet gone to the most remote parts. There were more local education authority schools in this province which often meant that tours of inspection did not take me as far afield. There was also more paperwork to contend with at the office in Broken Hill, where my detailed inspection reports and the fact that I actually sent copies of parts of them to the teachers and headmasters concerned staggered some of my colleagues. I actually heard one officer remark that he could not see why the teachers needed them! Apparently he did not realise that one of the main purposes of inspection was to let the teachers know where they could improve and to help them to do so.

In a town like Broken Hill, social life and the process of making new friends took a little longer to develop. Our circle expanded at a reasonable speed, especially since we had a foot in both the

Above: Livingstone's Fig Tree at Mwandi Mission, 1957. Livingstone camped under the tree in the 1850s. *Below:* The Land-Rover going on to the pontoon to cross the Zambesi at Sitoti, 1957.

Above: The royal Nalikwanda barge leaving Lealui, 1958. *Below:* Reroofing the house in Mongu in Barotseland, 1958.

Above: Setting out for fishing on Kamk Lake in Barotseland, 1958.
Below: Women dressed for the occasion at the Barotse Show, 1958.

Above: The Lozi Paramount Chief, Mwanawina III, on his way to his barge to leave Lealui at the Kuomboka in 1958. *Below:* Cattle by the Zambesi, Mongu, 1959.

Above: The young Kenneth Kaunda at a political rally in Broken Hill in the Central Province in 1960

Roy Welensky (Federal Prime Minister) and Harold Macmillan (British
Prime Minister) in Broken Hill in 1960.

Above: Village fruit sellers by the roadside near Mongu, 1959.
Below: Oxcart on the road near Kapila, Central Province, 1961.

Above: The Kariba Dam - not quite finished - in 1961. *Below:* The main road near Mkushi in the Central Province, 1961.

Above: Bridge on the road to Chalabesa Mission, Northern Province, 1962.
Below: The countryside near Fort Hill in Nyasaland in 1962.

Above: Elephant family in the Luangwa Valley, 1962. *Below:* Elephant invading Nsefu Camp in the Luangwa Valley, 1962.

Above: The wharf and the *Liemba* at Mpulungu in 1962. *Below:* Drying fish at Mpulungu on Lake Tanganyika, Northern Province, 1962.

Visit of the Parliamentary Secretary for Education to the Northern Province in March, 1964. At Mwenze Primary School in the Isoka District. The Headmaster, the Provincial Education Officer (the author), the Parliamentary Secretary, the Manager of Schools.

African and the European educational fields. The children soon adapted to the new type of school life, especially Brennian, who by nature was more gregarious than his sister, and they made friends quite quickly. We had left our puss, Frixos, with friends in Mongu when we set off on leave, and we now organised his transfer to Broken Hill. He came over from Mongu to Lusaka on the small plane, and he then travelled with me by road to Broken Hill (by this time Frixos was quite blasé about travelling). He immediately knew all of us, even after months of separation, and showed his great pleasure when we were reunited. He was also very good at adapting himself to new surroundings, never wandering far from the house; we never lost him, even for a night, though he always spent his nights outdoors, hunting and no doubt doing a bit of courting as well. In Broken Hill, however, a new presence was added to our household. One extremely wet night, when we had dinner guests with us, one of our guests asked us when we had got our dog. We looked blank, since we had no dog – or, at least, thought we hadn't – but we all trooped out to our front verandah, where, sure enough, sat a very large and friendly dog, whom I later identified with the help of the veterinary officer as a cross between a boxer and a great dane.

Buster, as he came to be called, arrived out of the dark and the rain and he stayed with us until we left Africa. We came to the conclusion that someone from the country, probably about to go away, had deliberately abandoned him in the town, perhaps hoping that someone would adopt him, just as we did. We made all the usual enquiries through the police and the S.P.C.A., but there was never any murmur of a claimant. Meanwhile, Buster stayed with us, becoming as attached to us as we, particularly the children, were to him. Frixos viewed this large four-legged phenomenon with some indignation at first and was quick to establish the fact that no dog, however large, was going to push him around on his own domain. But strangely enough a very good rapport was soon established; it was not long before they would sleep side by side, often with their backs touching, and they carefully respected each other. After a few weeks it was obvious that we could not send Buster away to someone else, even if anyone had appeared with an offer to take him, so Buster became one of the family for the next five years. After we had left Africa, I kept in touch with the people who took him over. He was again lucky to find a good home, and very much enhanced his reputation with his new owners when he fought and killed a baboon that attacked one of them. Baboons are unpleasant, vicious animals and there are few dogs that would even stay to fight one, let alone kill it. By the time that happened we were away in the Pacific in Western Samoa, but we still felt as proud of Buster as his new owners did.

By the beginning of 1961, it was obvious to all government officers that Britain was putting its weight on the side of those who wanted to see the Central African Federation broken up. Fortunately, as long as we were there in education or agriculture or whatever field, with our background of training and standards, and our separation from tribal pressures and therefore our recognised impartiality, African professional officers like teachers were not swayed by political events and continued to do their work well right up to the day of independence and afterwards. Once independence came, tribal influence and political expediency took over, and the teachers found themselves no longer free to devote themselves to their work as they had been able to before. Teachers did not often raise questions directly with an education officer on an inspection visit, other than questions that were purely about teaching, but they did quite frequently put questions through their headmasters, usually with a request that they should not be mentioned by name. The headmasters, however, usually told the education officer who had raised the question and asked in turn that the teacher's name should not be revealed. I always respected this request in any reports or correspondence or conversation, and I am pretty sure most European officers did. But even before independence one could never be quite certain of full confidentiality, especially if something was written down. Most P.E.O.s had European confidential secretaries, usually married ladies, often the wives of other government officers, and the ones I encountered were invariably very reliable, but, no matter how careful they were, the word 'confidential' on any document acts like a magnet. Then, as tends to happen anywhere, information was passed on with the usual injunction, 'Don't tell anyone, but I heard that – '. It was not surprising that teachers were afraid of their names being known, for some of the questions they asked involved policy and politics and the names of people who had power and influence. Most of us quickly adopted a policy of never writing down teachers' names in matters of this nature, keeping it between ourselves and the headmasters, who were usually reliable and generally appreciated the fact that we felt we could trust them. It did not always work, but the fact that it usually did spoke a great deal for the integrity of most of the headmasters, at least among those I encountered.

Our day-to-day work went on and we also enjoyed a good social life in Broken Hill. Our children were both at school and Hazel enjoyed her teaching. They all became involved in drama: the children in a junior group that put on some excellent shows; my wife in costumes for a production of James Elroy Flecker's *Hassan*, which proved outstanding, though the long hours of sewing and then helping at rehearsals, on top of daily school work, took a lot out of her. I started as part of the male chorus in a production of *The Mikado*, but pressure of work forced me to pull out of it after a few weeks. Broken Hill was very much alive in the amateur entertainment field and the Venus Theatre gave the community some remarkably good shows. In Barotseland, in a very small European community, our entertainment had been largely at the club and in individual dinner parties. In Broken Hill there were enough people to make much more public entertainment possible and people seemed to respond very well. Most Europeans, and quite a number of Indians and Africans, became involved in one way or another, a good thing for race relations on top of everything else.

Since coming to Northern Rhodesia, I had taken very little of the local leave that was due to me each year, preferring to wait for the long leaves overseas to visit home in New Zealand, or the United Kingdom and the Continent, but in August 1961 we took four or five days' leave to head for the Kafue game reserve. At that time the game reserves in Central Africa were all well controlled, as I hope they still are. Boundaries were well defined, fenced for many miles, with numerous check points and good camps for visitors. We stayed at two camps, at Chunga and at Ngoma, both very well organised with good accommodation. In the Kafue reserve, the visitor has to drive round well marked roads and is allowed to leave his car only at specified points. Once past the entry check point, we moved slowly and quietly as far as Chunga Camp, seeing plenty of wildlife along the way: warthog, sable antelope, impala, buffalo, many birds, and even a mongoose colony. We crossed the river by pontoon shortly before reaching the camp, where there was a fishing site which we also visited and tried out without any great success. There were various loop roads to follow and we made the most of those on the following day, moving on to the Ngoma Camp further north. Waterbuck, wildebeest and more buffalo – a herd of several hundred of them – were added to the list of what we saw. Game rangers did not travel with the visitor in the Kafue reserve, but were on constant patrol and in radio contact with one another. The next day we covered a further system of loop roads that gave us splendid views of eland, zebra, puku, and a lot of hippo. Only two animals eluded us completely on this trip: elephants and lions. Elephants are shrewd enough to keep out of the way with their excellent hearing and sense of smell, and lions seem to like keeping just ahead of tourists and out of sight, except for the occasional brief glimpse. The next day saw us heading back south on our way to leave the reserve. This took us most of the day, enabling us to see still more animals: hartebeest and kudu. The most numerous animals to be seen were buffalo, which move in quite large herds. They are, perhaps, the most sinister looking of animals and, as practised hunters will tell you, the most dangerous animal in Africa to hunt, more dangerous than elephant, lion, or leopard. Strangely enough, few leopards are seen in the game reserves; they move alone, or in very small family groups, and they move fast. A day later we were back in Broken Hill. I still have the list our children made of all the animals we saw; in most cases these included the actual number.

Later in the year, in December, we took another leave of just over a week to go south into Southern Rhodesia, which has since become Zimbabwe. We went first to Salisbury, now Harare, for a day or two. Salisbury was then a city of over 100,000 people, situated in much more open and cultivated country than any part of Northern Rhodesia: a very clean, bright place with some fine buildings and very good modern shops. I could see immediately why people in Southern Rhodesia referred to those from the Northern territory as 'cowboys from the wild north'. The highlights of Salisbury for the children were an excellent pantomime, *Puss in Boots*, and the film, *Ben Hur*. We took them to the latter with some misgivings, wondering how they would last out over the three hours of the film, but we need not have worried; they were fascinated and did not even want the two intervals to last as long as they did! We also visited a drive-in cinema, the first any of us had seen, and enjoyed a good Irish film and a snack meal in the car while we watched.

After Salisbury we moved out around the countryside, pausing at the famous Chrome Dyke, and eventually reaching the Sinoia caves, which we found very interesting, and quite different from either the Waitomo caves in New Zealand or the Jenolan caves in Australia. Our next stop was Kariba and its dam, a magnificent piece of engineering. It had just been completed at the time we saw it, but was still undergoing work at one end where some rock movement had been detected. The dam was built by an Italian firm, who had built a special church for their Italian workers: a beautifully designed and appointed circular building, at that time already a showpiece for visitors to Kariba. Kariba was an attractive spot in many ways, but, situated deep in a narrow valley and gorge, it was hot and sticky, not a place we would have wanted to live in for long. Once across the dam we were back in Northern Rhodesia and on our way home – finding, incidentally, the Northern roads outside the towns far better than those in the South. The year 1961 ended on a happy note for us personally, with a pleasant, but busy Christmas, with nine adults and six children sitting down to a quite hilarious Christmas dinner. The new year came in quietly, turning into a very wet January after the first few days.

I began the year by touring in the Western area around Mumbwa, a part of the country we had recently passed through on our way to the Kafue game reserve, but the rains had now descended and I spent my time slithering and sliding through a sea of mud from one rural school to the next. It was often easier to move off the road and drive through the scrub and trees than it was to plough through what was designated the road. I came back to Broken Hill in time to be there for the junior drama presentation of several short plays in which our children and their friends were all taking part. In fact, Brennian managed to distinguish himself as Mr Fish, a teacher, in one play, earning some very good comment in the local paper and showing in his performance the quick wit that is still very much a part of him. Then I got the surprise of my life. On the telephone from Lusaka came one of the great men himself. I had been promoted to senior education officer, the promotion back-dated to the middle of 1961. For once the Biscuit Factory had dumbfounded me!

There were only eight S.E.O.s in Northern Rhodesia and, as far as I had been able to see, I had very little chance of becoming one of them. I had no public school background, no old school tie, and, although born in England, by my own choice I was designated a New Zealander, a colonial. I could see that I had done my job well, but I had also trodden on one or two of the wrong toes. However, there were people in the department, even in Lusaka, who looked beyond those things and they had clearly decided that I was at least worth a try in one of these senior jobs. With the news of promotion came the information that I was appointed provincial education officer of the Northern Province and was to move up to Kasama before the end of the month. At one and the same time we were elated and despondent; I had promotion and was a permanent senior officer, but Kasama had no European school. The children had just got settled at school in Broken Hill, so to thrust them on to a correspondence course was far from desirable. We considered it from all angles. I knew the Southern Province also had a vacancy, with its headquarters in Livingstone, a town very similar to Broken Hill, complete with European primary and secondary schools, but my enquiry in that respect met a blank wall. The wheels had turned and could not be turned back; bureaucratic rigidity, as almost anywhere, prevailed. No postings could possibly be changed. So we sat down as a family and decided that Hazel and the children must stay in Broken Hill and I would go alone to Kasama. Our next leave was due in August, 1963, so we reckoned that, with visits whenever possible, we could survive living apart for the next twenty months. The children could carry on their schooling undisturbed and, with Hazel continuing to teach, we could run two households successfully. It had its grim aspects, but we put those aside and we managed.

A new P.E.O. had already arrived for the Central Province, so my period as acting P.E.O. was over there. This meant moving away presented few problems as far as my work was concerned, but I had to move swiftly to get the family organised in Broken Hill in a matter of about ten days. We occupied our present government housing by virtue of my position in the African education department; once I was posted elsewhere, the house had to be vacated. What I did with my family was my concern. In very quick time, through friends with whom we still communicate to this day, we got hold of quite a sizeable flat on the second floor of a block that was conveniently placed for the schools, and the family were soon organised into it. My move was so sudden that we had no large farewell parties. On 29 January I quietly left Broken Hill, having seen Hazel and the children off to their schools. Frixos stayed with the family in the flat; Buster sat between me and my driver in the Land-Rover, heading north for a new home, almost five hundred miles away.

That day saw the end of my time in Broken Hill and the Central Province after just under a year and a half there. For the next four years my concern was the Northern Province, the subject of the next section of this account. Looking back over the time I had spent in Broken Hill, even just after I had moved north, I could see that it had been basically a good time. It was an unsettled period in many ways, but by then everyone, European and African alike, was unsettled, because there was no certainty as to the future. The British government seemed to work on a system of keeping people in the dark for as long as possible. They apparently believed that, if they did that, people would continue to devote themselves to the job in hand, because there was no official word of any change. To some extent, of course, this worked. People did shrug and say, 'Let's wait and see', and got on with their work. But they seethed inside.

Various ministers in the Northern Rhodesian government were already Africans by now, and education was always a field where the government felt Africans were needed: a sensible enough idea, since territorial education concerned African education only. In the Central Province we had an official ministerial visit in May 1961, something no one ever relished greatly. The P.E.O. asked me as his deputy to be with him throughout the official visit, which lasted two or three days, so I was there with him and the minister throughout. At first we found the minister aloof and very guarded, obviously suspicious that we somehow did not approve of him, but after the first day he began to relax. I think perhaps he realised that we were interested in education far more than we were in politics, and that, as long as he showed interest and a desire to further the cause of education for the African, we did not care what political party he belonged to nor was it particularly important to us whether he was an African or a European. The visit ended on a very good note in a friendly atmosphere; the Minister was no longer the dour, remote, unsmiling man who arrived, but left us smiling and talking freely and easily. As he moved off, I remember the P.E.O. and I looking at each other, grinning, and both putting our thumbs up. We knew that the visit had been a success.

But the mood in the country was darkening, with a real threat of armed struggle rather than a calm, peaceful transition to independence. There was trouble in the Northern Province, the stronghold of the United National Independence Party, during 1961, clearly organised by the party, and this spread into the eastern end of the Central Province, without, fortunately, ever becoming a major threat. In the towns there was no real trouble to speak of: drunken brawling on a fairly large scale rather than organised rioting or anything like terrorist attacks. The police were able to keep a firm hold, but I think one of the main reasons for the comparative peace in Northern Rhodesia was the fact that the majority of Africans, regardless of their tribe, just wanted to get on with their daily lives and be left in peace to do so.

Our divided family life took some getting accustomed to, but we all adapted quickly. Our children, at the ages of twelve and just coming up to eleven, slipped into the new pattern readily, largely because their school life was not disturbed. They did not realise at the time the strain it placed on their parents, but we were determined to make it work until we went on leave in 1963. For some time we had been making enquiries in New Zealand on the best boarding schools, and had decided that the children would remain in New Zealand after this leave. We could have sent them to Southern Rhodesia or to South Africa quite satisfactorily, but we wanted them to realise that they were New Zealanders. Enquiries with the colonial service showed that we could get government assistance to fly them out to us for at least the long school holiday each year. Meanwhile we carried on as we were, with three quarters of the family and the cat in Broken Hill, and the dog and myself in Kasama. We launched into copious correspondence, of course, with regular letters each week. My wife even helped me to organise the Kasama garden by correspondence, complete with diagrams for the lay-out and schedules for planting, etc. I still have some of those letters. During most school holidays, the family came up to Kasama, and Hazel became an expert at negotiating the corrugated dirt roads at speed. She made the four hundred and fifty mile journey in one day, often with not only our own children on board, but also those of other government officers in Kasama. On one occasion she brought herself and seven children up; looking back, I can see that those journeys were something of an achievement. Usually I managed to organise my touring so that I could get myself down to the border of the province to meet the car, a great occasion for all of us when each vehicle was spotted through the red dust or in the mud. From there we would travel with the car following my Land-Rover, Brennian and one of the boys often in the Land-Rover with me, while my driver slept happily in the back of the vehicle for the two-hundred miles back to Kasama. Those trips are something none of us have ever forgotten.

In Kasama and later, I was able to reflect on our Broken Hill days and what, perhaps, we had learned from them. In Mongu we had grown to appreciate the vastness of Africa and how small an impression man had actually made upon it. It also seemed that we had seen the African at his best out there: courteous, dignified, in close communion with his world around him, secure in his tribal organisation and life. Here, in what was termed civilisation, we saw the African unsettled, often uprooted, unsure of himself, loosened from his tribal links, and beset by the temptations of all the paraphernalia of 'civilisation' he saw around him. One wondered whether this civilisation was such a good thing after all. But it also brought home to us once again that the changes we saw taking place were inevitable. Sooner or later it was bound to come. There was no way Africa could remain isolated.

Broken Hill gave us personally more physical comfort and convenience; it solved our schooling problems and made living easier. But it also tended to remove some of the close touch we had with the African people themselves. Fortunately I still had some remote areas to cope with in the Central Province, and from time to time I still found that spirit of Africa there, but we were never quite as close to the Africans again as we had been in Barotseland. The Broken Hill days were good days and good for our children, for they brought them back much nearer to what for them would be normal life in the future. We made a lot of friends in Broken Hill and found the social life and the variety of entertainment very enjoyable. I suppose our time there balanced things up again, so to speak, placing us in a style of life somewhere between the rather rigid divisions of the Copperbelt towns and the government-orientated life of the remote Zambesi country. Here we had mixed freely with Europeans from all walks of life, with Indians, and with sophisticated Africans.

For me, the centre of operations had now moved between four- and five-hundred miles further north and my thinking was being reorientated once again. For the family, their centre was still Broken Hill for daily living, and they were all kept busy both in their work and in their recreation. It was after I had gone up to Kasama that the Federal Broadcasting Organisation became interested in some of my short stories and several of them were read over the air. I was one of comparatively few Northern Rhodesian contributors to what was predominantly a Southern Rhodesian service. But it was a Federal service and, when the Federation finally dissolved, its broadcasting became a purely Southern concern, while the Northern service became virtually African, and for Africans. Two of my stories that made a strong impression in Northern Rhodesia are reproduced later in this work. In spite of the separation and the problems this presented, 1962 moved on well and I felt that I was at last getting somewhere, after about fifteen years in the colonial service, a service I enjoyed and of which I was proud to be a part, though I did not always enjoy all the people I encountered in it.

Time rolled on towards our next leave, and the only change we made to our pattern was to transfer Frixos up to Kasama, where he had a much more pleasant home than in the flat in Broken Hill. Otherwise life went on, and we grew reasonably accustomed to our separation into two households, knowing that the time would soon come when it ended – at least for the two of us. But it would also mean separation from our children for the first time.

6

The Northern Marches

The Northern Province was a vast area, almost 60,000 square miles, and for educational purposes it was divided into two sections, both provinces, the Northern and the Luapula regions. The Northern region, which became my territory, was more than 50,000 square miles, while the Luapula region was a much smaller strip to the west, centred on Fort Rosebery. My headquarters and new home were at Kasama, now on the Tanzam Railway, which links Zimbabwe, Zambia and Tanzania, an uneconomic line built for political purposes in an attempt to avoid going through South Africa. Political acts of this nature are inevitable, but they have cost new African states – or their sponsors – a lot of money in many parts of the continent. For comparison, the area I had to cover was approaching the size of England and Wales together in the United Kingdom, or nearly the size of the entire South Island, New Zealand. Even as provincial education officer, this meant a lot of travelling, though fortunately the whole area was high and, in general, not too difficult for vehicles even in the wet season.

Most of the province lay in the red or red-brown earth region, the soil being reasonably fertile, so the rural population was better off for food production than it had been in Barotseland, though the land was not perhaps as good as that around Broken Hill. The entire area was high, ranging from just under 4,000 feet to over 7,000 feet. The land reached its highest on the Nyika plateau, a rocky, open area with few trees, in the north towards the Tanzanian border. The countryside in general was rolling hills, a type of tree savannah, the trees being rather stunted, with scrub and grass below them. There were frequent open stretches, called pans or *vleis*, flat and hard in the dry season, often becoming shallow lakes during the rains. Grass grew abundantly in all the open areas, often reaching a height of six or eight feet. With infrequent traffic, especially off the main routes, the grass shot up everywhere except on the vehicle tracks, so the traveller was often faced with six feet and more of coarse grass on either side and in the centre of the roadway. All he could do was follow the vehicle tracks, pushing down the grass ahead of him. It then sprang up again behind him, of course, so he had to carry on surrounded by a sea of grass. For some reason African drivers enjoyed this and delighted in roaring along at about forty miles an hour, which was fine - unless there happened to be an outcrop of rock in the middle off the road or a tree fallen across it, when the car came to a very abrupt halt. I managed to keep my drivers down to about twenty miles an hour in such country, striking fallen trees on a couple of occasions without damage to either vehicle or person. One interesting sideline emerged from this. I had been brushing up my Cibemba and was interested to hear some lurid swearing from my driver, who obviously thought I did not know what he was saying. Not much further on, we struck yet another hole in the road and both hit the roof of the vehicle cab. I uttered a couple of his choice Cibemba words. There was an acute and embarrassed silence while my driver cautiously looked round at me. After a few seconds I grinned at him and nodded. He shook his head in that very characteristic African fashion, putting his hand to his forehead. Then we both burst out laughing and could not stop for about half a mile.

The Northern Province is the heart of the Bemba country. The tribe probably moved in from the west across the Luapula river round about 1700 and the settlement of Kasama has been there, more or less on the same spot, for three centuries and more. It is a pity Africans there did not erect permanent buildings, as happened in Zimbabwe; if they had, we would have a more certain and authenticated history in many places. However, their way of life, the struggle they often had just to survive, their shortage of building materials and their lack of tools made such development near to impossible. The same was unfortunately the case with the

Polynesian and Melanesian peoples in the Pacific, although in New Zealand the materials for permanency were there but were simply not utilised.

The first Europeans to appear in Northern Rhodesia were the Portuguese. As early as 1505 they had taken the settlement of Sofala on the Mozambique coast and made it one of their main stations on the route to India. Their first ventures into the interior seem to have been made in about 1511, when they probed into what is now Zimbabwe. It was also, in fact, called Zimbabwe then, part of the Monomatapa empire. The main objective of the Portuguese was the search for gold, and when no great discoveries were made and reports arrived of gold in the East Indies, their interest declined. Some Portuguese interest still remained, though, since they needed coastal staging points on the route to India, and from time to time fresh probes were made into the interior. The coastal stations served to provide fresh fruit and vegetables to the ships passing back and forth round the Cape, and both East and Central Africa owed the presence of such thing as sweet potatoes, onions, lentils, guavas, pawpaws, oranges and lemons to the Portuguese, who brought them to their settlements from India and the Far East. During the seventeenth century, a Goanese named Pereira penetrated the Zambesi valley as far as the junction with the Luangwa river and established the settlement of Zumbo – where I had bought my Portuguese wine in 1961. However, the Portuguese do not seem to have penetrated Northern Rhodesia until late in the eighteenth century, by which time they were involved in the slave trade both alongside, and in competition with, the Arabs. In 1827 they set up a military post in the Lundazi district in the north-eastern corner of Northern Rhodesia, part of the Northern Province, but they withdrew from there after only two years. By this time, 'black ivory', the name used to denote the slaves who were traded in, was more important than gold in this part of the world, but this trade was largely in the hands of the Arabs. There is no record of the Portuguese actually reaching Kasama, but it is possible they may have done so.

The nineteenth century saw a great deal of European movement into the area of the Rhodesias, the most prominent figure, of course, being David Livingstone, but his travels took him mostly back and forth further south, not in the area which was to become the Northern Province. From about 1800 onwards, missionaries began to make their way north from South Africa, mostly British in the early days, since the Cape area had been taken over by the British. Livingstone made one notable foray from Nyasaland, now Malawi, right across the Northern Province, reaching Lake Tanganyika in April 1867, spending some time thereafter exploring round Lakes Mweru and Bangweulu, and it was just south of this area that he eventually died in 1873. The number of missions operating steadily multiplied as the years went by. In the Northern Province, the year 1885 was notable for the foundation of the ill-fated London Missionary Society mission at Niamkolo near Mpulungu at the southern end of Lake Tanganyika. The mission was eventually abandoned after years of constant struggle with Arab slave traders, disease, isolation, and vacillating support from the Africans in the region. The ruins of mission buildings, and what was intended to be a magnificent church, are still there. The church was never finished.

Kasama appeared on the map, so to speak, when the British South Africa Company established a post there in 1899. The Company administration actually continued in Northern Rhodesia until 1924, although from 1911 it was under considerable Crown control. Prior to 1899 there had been a good deal of tribal and factional fighting in the area, but the presence of a recognised authority brought that to an abrupt halt after one or two sharp clashes. At least as far as Europeans were concerned, Kasama was the centre of the Northern Province from that time onwards. When I went there in 1962, the provincial administration had been operating from there for almost forty years and there was no question, even in African minds, that this was the provincial capital. The township lies along the side of quite a notable hill in this rolling country not noted for many outstanding features. Even from the north, where the country rises fairly steadily, one still has to climb a hill to come into Kasama. It is not a large place, nothing like the size of Broken Hill or Chingola or Ndola, but it is, or was then, well provided with facilities: a post office, a bank, a number of shops, a garage, and, of course, fairly extensive government offices, embracing all the various departments. These were not all in one place, however, and my offices were immediately behind my house. I could walk to work in about two minutes and go to my office after hours whenever I felt inclined, which, when I was in Kasama alone, I frequently did. Immediately in front of my house was the golf course, quite an extensive and well tended one, and the road where my house stood stretched in a gentle curve for half a mile or more to the club, the centre of much European social life. Many European houses were down the length of this road, all sharing a pleasant outlook on to the golf course.

My house was actually at one end of the course and we always kept a water bag hanging under a tree beside our drive entrance. There was a green and a tee just opposite across the road, so golfers could pause for a drink before teeing off for the homeward journey. In fact, quite often they ran for shelter on our verandah if a sudden storm caught them, as could easily happen in the wet season. There was quite a sizeable garden with numerous tall trees and a large clump of well-developed bamboo, which unfortunately was a great haven for snakes. Down one side of the house were mango trees, a magnet for African boys. Our dog, Buster, was a great asset here; he made a dreadful noise, but never bit anyone, so I simply let him out, if I heard youthful voices round the side of the house. I am sure some African boys became good hurdlers, judging by the way they used to clear the stone wall and hare off down the road, dropping most of their mangoes on the way. Every now and then we pretended we had not heard them, kept Buster inside, and let them take their fruit, for we usually had plenty when we wanted it. I got the garden started – by correspondence with my wife! – before the family were able to join me and they were still in Broken Hill. It was very successful and Hazel was able to put right whatever I had done wrong and set me on course for the next term when the family came up in the school holidays. I also got hens organised in a good strong hen-run; there were leopards, hyenas and wild dogs in the area, though only a couple of times did we have any round the house, since they generally kept well away from any settlement. Incredible numbers of birds, however, at first enjoyed the hen food as much as the hens, until I covered the hen-run with wire.

As the provincial education officer, I was not expected to tour as much, but, especially when I first arrived in the province, I wanted to know my territory as much as possible at first hand, so I went out into the bush a good deal. I had left Broken Hill at the end of January arriving in Kasama on the 30th, which I felt was an auspicious day to arrive, since it happened to be my parents' wedding anniversary. Just one week later we had a visit from the governor, then Sir Evelyn Hone. One of the first official visits he made was to the trades' school at Lukashya, just a mile or two from Kasama, and I, of course, had to be there. The next day the governor visited the secondary school at Mungwi about twelve miles out, and again I had to be there. I was also now a member of what was known as the provincial team, a gathering each month of all the heads of departments and the district commissioners under the chairmanship of the provincial commissioner. That same afternoon the provincial team met to be addressed by the governor, while in the evening we all had to gather at the provincial commissioner's house to meet His Excellency, socially. So in a couple of days I saw a great deal of the governor. Strangely enough, out at the schools he seemed at ease and talked readily, but over a drink he seemed to freeze up. He was most difficult to talk with because he left you to lead the conversation, a most unusual thing for a man in his position to do. Even the provincial commissioner found the same thing and, after I had been guided to the governor for my little session of conversation, the P.C., whom I had known for some years, grinned at me and said, 'Head still above water, I see!' 'Just!' I replied, feeling this to be very true.

The European staff at Education headquarters consisted of the P.E.O. (myself), two education officers (one man and one woman), an accountant, a secretary (who was a married lady), and a trades training supervisor. At that stage I had no African E.O. or assistant, but there was a good manager of schools and the usual complement of African clerks, messengers, drivers, etc. It was a good staff and I quickly found that we worked well together. As well as European administrative and inspecting staff, there were European principals at the secondary schools and the trades' school. African staff were being increased rapidly at these institutions now that independence was in sight, and I later got an excellent African E.O., who was ultimately to become my replacement. The main problem, as had been the case for some time, was to find enough properly qualified Africans to take posts in the inspectorate and the secondary schools. Standards in primary education were rising, but the required qualifications there were not as high as in the secondary schools, where there were plenty of good, experienced men moving up steadily. Finding qualified African women officers was an even greater problem right up to and after independence, though good material was moving through the teachers' colleges all over the country. Time was, of course, the great factor. A teacher cannot be trained satisfactorily in less than two years, and trainees must have a reasonable basic education to start with. We needed teachers, especially women, every year, and they were just not emerging quickly enough. The most encouraging sign for the future was the way the teachers themselves responded when they understood what we were trying to do and the problems we faced. Standards rose not because more teachers were put into the schools and classes reduced in size - although this was done as far as was possible – but because the existing teachers, or at least most of them, put their backs into their work with an energy that surprised most Europeans and a lot of senior Africans as well.

At about the time of the governor's visit to the Northern Province, new service conditions in the colonial service were announced to allay the growing unrest among expatriate officers. These conditions were such that it made staying on in Northern Rhodesia worthwhile until independence came. Then, in March, the new Northern Rhodesian constitution was made public. Not surprisingly it pleased no one totally because it had to be something of a compromise, satisfying everyone to some extent: the African nationalist, the African moderate, the British government, the existing Northern Rhodesian government, world opinion, the Americans and the United Nations. Hence, it was hardly surprising that it ended up a rather strange mixture. However, at least with our service conditions clear, and the constitutional path now defined as far as was possible, we more or less knew where we stood and could regulate our efforts accordingly. Even though we might not agree with all that was set out before us, at last we could steer a proper course. There was a great feeling of relief, despite caustic comments and wry jokes about the future. Everyone began to look further afield and, as far as I was concerned, my interest lay in the Pacific, for next time we went on leave we would be placing our children at boarding schools in New Zealand – and Africa was a long way off. But leave was still more than a year away and the tentative independence deadline more than two years. I would then have the option of staying on for six months after independence to decide whether I wanted to continue working for the new government on a contract basis, in all probability for two years at a time. However, I was not optimistic about the way African thought was moving. In conversation with an African politician at a function during an education conference in Lusaka I was told, 'We shall still need Europeans, but we shall prefer new faces. You chaps, you old hands know too much about us.' And this had been said before the end of 1962.

Our normal work went on, and, as far as I could see, most European officers, no matter what department they might be in, kept steadily working on, determined that they would go out in due course on a high note. For my part, I was kept very busy; in my first six or seven months in the province I had a senior education officers' conference in Lusaka, teachers' refresher courses in my own territory in June, a school managers' course in July, all interspersed with some extensive touring to familiarise myself with my distinctly extensive territory, as well as the normal paperwork in my office. I was lucky in the quality of my assistants, male and female, and the affairs of the province ran smoothly, with, of course, the usual occasional upheavals. So far politics did not intrude too much into the schools, but inevitably it did affect the teachers in varying degrees. The United National Independence Party was very strongly supported by the Bemba people and this area was their homeland, so some attempts were made to exert influence in the schools and even in my offices in Kasama. In the early stages both the political agitators and the teachers were cautious, but later, in the last months before independence, these attempts naturally became bolder and louder. There were even outspoken personal attacks on European officers as well as on senior Africans. Attempts were made to oust several of my best

African headmasters, my provincial accountant, and my trades training supervisor. I managed to get round all this by inviting UNIP officials to my office to talk. Rather surprisingly they came and we discussed matters in a reasonably friendly and peaceful manner, parting on quite good terms. After this, we encountered no more personal assaults of fiery rhetoric, much to everyone's relief.

My diary contains frequent comments to the effect that our headquarters in Lusaka often did not seem to know what went on in the provinces. That happens everywhere, of course, and every P.E.O. must have felt irritated and frustrated at times when letters from Lusaka dwelt on trivialities while virtually ignoring what to him were the vital issues. Things usually got sorted out in the end, but sometimes it took a lot of time and a lot of paper. The telephone was there, but connections were often bad; one heard only half of what was said or was cut off in the middle of a conversation. We often used to joke that the 'bush telegraph' was quicker, just as accurate, and often more so. It was curious how African clerks could often me tell things days before I received any official word, like a coming visit from one of the boffins or an overseas visitor. More than once surprise visits by senior gentlemen from headquarters were foiled, so to speak, by the bush telegraph. Although I already knew they were coming – though not perhaps the exact day – I always tried not to make this obvious, but usually someone inadvertently let the cat out of the bag. Among the senior officers with a sense of humour – and there were a number of them – it became a joke that I operated a spy network that stretched to Lusaka more than five hundred miles away.

Touring in the Northern Province was perhaps more interesting than elsewhere and yet sometimes tedious because of the distances involved. The general lie of the land from Kasama was a rise to the north, north-east, and east, the main eastern centres being Chinsali and Isoka. To the west there was a downward slope to the centres of Luwingu and Mporokoso, the former about ninety miles due west, the latter some hundred and twenty miles north-west. Beyond that the land began to sink towards the Congo basin, with the Luapula area marking the beginning of the real central African rain forest. Up around Kasama we were on the surrounding rim of the basin and hence there was a difference in landscape and vegetation. We had three big lakes or parts of them in this northern part of Northern Rhodesia: Tanganyika, about a hundred miles north of Kasama; Bangweulu, about a hundred miles south-west; and Mweru, about a hundred and fifty miles north-west. Bangweulu, across the Morfu swamplands, and Mweru, fed by the Luapula river, were both outside my provincial education region, but the southern end of Tanganyika down below Abercorn, (now called Mbala), the most northerly centre in the province, came well within it.

Perhaps here in the north, more than anywhere else in Northern Rhodesia, I got an impression of the vastness of Africa. Stopping by the roadside somewhere off the main routes, I was conscious first of the silence and then, after a short time, of the fact that it was not actually silence. There were always sounds of which I gradually became aware, many of them sounds I could not define. Often the absence of man and his works, however humble or primitive, was striking; I really was miles from anywhere and, because the land was more open, I could see much further, which added to my awareness of the vastness of this African landscape. I remember stopping once on my way home from a tour of inspection to get a photograph of the setting sun, a red ball in the smoke of a grass fire, apparently setting between distant trees. It turned out to be a very good photograph. My map told me that I was just over thirty miles past the last village and still sixty miles from the main road back to Kasama. No other settlement appeared on my map within forty miles of where I stopped to take that photo. If one's vehicle broke down in places like this, it could be a long wait until someone happened to come along one of these side roads, so I was always prepared with the necessary gear and some emergency supplies, but sooner or later a mission truck or another government vehicle would roll up, maybe within an hour, maybe on the following day. I was lucky that I never got stuck in this way, but we once towed a police Land-Rover forty miles to its base and earned the undying gratitude of a young European officer who had been in the country for less than a year and the African constable who was his driver. They would have done the same for me, if the position had been reversed. On tour we always carried everything: repair outfits, more than one spare tyre, a full drum of petrol, and towing gear.

In addition to the two education officers stationed with me in Kasama, I had a third in Chinsali, who looked after a big eastern strip of the province, and a fourth, an African, who operated from Abercorn. Without these men in areas away from Kasama, we could never have covered the ground and kept our eyes on the schools in an adequate manner. The 'bush telegraph' operated out there, too, of course, and once I had left my headquarters, or, at least, as soon as I reached the first school on my list, the word was out. I was never quite sure exactly how, because there were no telephones to villages or bush schools. In Barotseland the Africans had still made use of drums which often pounded through the night. Up here in the north, one heard them much less frequently, largely because distances were greater, often too great even for the penetrating sound of the African drum. No other group of people I have ever come across, even in the Pacific, can speak with drums the way Africans can, but even their powers have limits.

The bush school often had very little around it, maybe only one or two huts, but there was always a village within a mile or so, although school pupils would come from much further afield and, as in most parts of the territory, would walk miles daily to get to school and back. Once I visited a school where only just over half those enrolled were present; on enquiry I found that all the absentees came from two villages nearly ten miles away, but there was a pride of lions settled on the track between them and the school. No one dared to come through until the lions moved on, which they did a day or two after I had visited the school. Nobody treats lions lightly, least of all those who understand the wildlife so well.

By the time the end of the year was approaching, I had managed to get to every district in the province and had made myself known to a great many teachers. I still followed the pattern of making individual reports and I got my education officers to produce similar reports when they went out on inspection. One of them was obviously not keen on the idea and did what I asked with some reluctance; the others saw the value of such reports and produced them readily and fully. As in other places, the headmasters and the teachers themselves clearly appreciated the system. My African successor, I know, intended to carry on the scheme, but whether he was able to do so in the face of all the political pressures that came in after independence I do not know. Africans generally prefer not to commit things to paper; they tend to fear the written word as being too definite, too hard to deny later, and difficult to get around. The members of my family were surviving our enforced separation well, looking forward from one school holiday to the next. Despite the long drive up from Broken Hill, the family loved Kasama with our big house and garden, the openness and the freedom, and the presence of Frixos and Buster (Frixos came up to stay on the first family visit in April). In August, however, I again took some local leave, and this time we all set off on what I consider to be our best trip in Africa, ten days of touring round the Eastern Province, the Luangwa valley, a little of Malawi, the Nyika plateau, and finally home to Kasama for the rest of the school holiday.

In my time in Africa I saw a lot of wildlife, especially with all my journeying off the main roads and often right through the bush, following no road at all. Nowhere else, however, did I see it quite as I did in the Luangwa valley. It was a great experience, something that none of my family will ever forget. The time to go to a game reserve is, of course, in the dry season, so we went in August, when, though it could be cloudy and was often very cool at night, there was no chance of any rain. We had arranged to set off from Broken Hill and, since I had official business to take me to Ndola, I flew from Kasama via Fort Rosebery to Ndola, did what I had to do there, and was then given a lift to Broken Hill by a friend late the same afternoon. The four of us set off in our own car the next morning, heading through Lusaka, pausing to see friends at Munali secondary school before heading off into new territory. We crossed the Luangwa River about a hundred and thirty miles from Lusaka and were then in the Eastern Province, where the first thing that struck us was how poor the roads were. We coped with this, despite the appalling corrugations, since we were accustomed to dealing with these on parts of the Northern Province roads. Another hundred miles saw us at the small settlement of Petauke, where we spent the night in a rather scruffy government rest house.

We survived that, moving on the next morning on rather better roads to reach the main Eastern Province centre, Fort Jameson, another hundred miles east, just before midday. We had never been in this area before and found the differences interesting; the road actually runs along a ridge, the land falling away steeply to the south into what is, in fact, part of the Rift valley.

We were quite impressed with Fort Jameson, a neat little settlement with pleasant surroundings, more hilly than Kasama, but we were keen to get on our way into the game reserve. We made a quick call on friends, both doctors, before pushing on, this time back westwards on the road that led to the Luangwa valley, a typical dirt road, corrugated and dusty. We passed through the control point early in the afternoon, and by mid-afternoon were getting settled in the Nsefu camp, a well-organised and well-appointed place with very pleasant rondavel accommodation, well protected from ants, bats, rats, and numerous night insects. Even before we reached the camp, we paused to watch a herd of elephant and numerous zebra, wildebeest and impala. After our evening meal, while it was still light, an elephant came right up to the camp and we all spent nearly an hour watching his leisurely antics.

Once in the camp, the recognised procedure was to arrange with the game ranger in charge to go out on foot with a game guard. Parties were limited to four people with one guard, so next morning, at about 6 a.m., we set off with a game guard all to ourselves, a very pleasant and skilful African who obviously knew what he was doing. All guards carried rifles – just in case – but they were very rarely used. They knew approximately where various animals would be found from day to day, so we drove with our guard to recognised and protected parking spots, left our vehicle there, and walked for an hour or two in the bush. That first morning we walked for more than two hours amongst innumerable impala, puku, water buck, and many elephants. The great thing about this practice was that we moved quietly on foot and the wildlife for the most part were not alarmed by our presence. This made for wonderful photography. The animals and birds were living normal and natural lives, but were protected as far as possible from that most appalling of predators: man. We finished our first jaunt at about nine, and rested around the camp until about three, when we set off again for another two hour walk with our guard, Michael, who obviously liked the children and seemed to enjoy having just one family with him. This time we suddenly came face to face with a large rhino, who eyed us fixedly and pawed the ground with one foot. 'Just stand!' Michael whispered and we did. I think we were just about paralysed anyway. There were no trees around, only long grass and anthills, so we just stood and waited. I carefully took two photos from about twenty yards. The rhino seemed to hear even the faint click of the camera, gave a loud snort, and suddenly galloped off to be lost from sight in the high grass, while we all struggled to get our breathing back to normal. A little later on our way back to Nsefu in the car, a large elephant objected to our presence and began to move out on to the road with distinct aggression. However, I swung off the road round a clump of trees and made off before he had time to get any closer. That evening we had several hippo and some buffalo right up at the edge of the camp.

The next day saw us make another early start, this time on the lookout for lions. We found a pair, but they knew we were there and led us around for some seven miles. I never got my photographs of them. They kept between fifty and a hundred yards ahead of us all the time, seeming to take a delight in showing themselves, usually just a head or head and shoulders, from time to time around a bush or a rock or an anthill. We enjoyed the chase and I think the lions did also! Eventually they just left us and disappeared into the bush. In the course of all this, we came upon a large rhino fast asleep under a tree, stretched out very peacefully. We walked quietly past, not even taking a photo, in case he awoke. Back at the camp and ready for a rest, we spent an hour or more watching two elephants stroll right through the camp within a few yards of our huts, treating everyone with lofty disdain and eventually wandering off into the bush in a very confident and leisurely manner. Our afternoon session took us into another area, where we saw some magnificent kudu, probably the finest looking of all the different types of buck. They are tall and powerful with most elegant blue markings on their coats. Under the moon at night, a lame hippo, who had established himself in the river beside the camp, came right up under the bank below us to disport himself with much snorting and blowing.

Next morning, early as usual, we set off on our last Nsefu walk, another three hour trek. It was again well worth the effort and we saw a great deal, at one stage walking right into a big herd of buffalo. At first we could see only three or four, but Michael murmured, 'Many, many,' pointing with his chin in true African style, and we soon saw many, probably in all about two hundred of them. Michael signalled us to move quietly back; we were happy to do so. These most sinister looking animals stood in a semi-circle around us, watching without sound or movement. They were the only things we met on the bush walks that scared us, as the buffalo has been known to hunt the hunter quite frequently, and also has a nasty habit, once it has knocked you down, of kneeling on you! We looked back every few minutes, and even at about three hundred yards the buffalo all still stood motionless, watching us. By that time we were far enough away to quicken our pace and get right out of the area. Just after lunch we said goodbye to Michael and to Nsefu and set off for a more northerly camp at Luambe. I often wonder what became of Michael after independence, hoping that he stayed on in the game department, doing his job as a game guard and guide that he did so very well and pleasantly. On the way to Luambe we stopped two or three times to watch various animals and birds, but we did not leave the car. We finally reached Luambe in about the middle of the afternoon.

The camp there was not as good as that at Nsefu, but pleasant enough, although the accommodation was rather crowded since the huts were much smaller. We watched some buck from the camp and some baboons, the first we had seen in the reserve. Next morning we went off for more than two hours with a very young African game guard, a nice enough man, but lacking Michael's skill and knowledge. We saw numerous animals taking their early morning drink, including a number of elephant, and walked through some considerably thicker, but very pleasant, bush. We left the Luangwa valley reserve after lunch on our way to Lundazi, where we were able to stay at the famous – or perhaps notorious – Castle Hotel, a magnificent place built like a small castle and very well appointed and run: a favourite tourist spot even in those days.

I think half its attraction lay in the stories of how it had been built by a district commissioner by the name of Button between 1947 and 1952. One version had it that, when told to build a new building for his district offices, he had produced the castle, which was virtually a fortress. People maintained that he could not possibly have produced this on the funds voted for it alone, and that he had regularly diverted extra funds from other sources under his control. Maybe he did manage to re-direct some funds now and again, but it would have been a very difficult task. My own experience was that the great men in Lusaka, and especially those in the Treasury, reacted very slowly and reluctantly to most requests and followed up the results equally slowly – unless the spending of money was involved. They then very quickly wanted to know where every last penny had gone, once the money had been voted. Nothing galvanised them into action more quickly than a need to account for money used and, if the recovery of money for an overpayment was required, they could move with lightning speed. Payment of money out, or arrears for an underpayment, was a different matter: this could take months. However he had managed it, Button succeeded in building his castle that ultimately became the Castle Hotel, and he made a most attractive job of it. We found the hotel pleasant in service and surroundings, despite the presence of a team of American 'do-gooders' who had been in Nyasaland, a singularly scruffy and untidy collection of juveniles, who were very similar to some of the British V.S.O. personnel we endured from time to time in Northern Rhodesia. We were able to avoid the American group in Lundazi, who spent much of their time loudly talking to one another about what 'these British' had done in Nyasaland. Looking back now, I am reminded of a later encounter with the American Peace Corps in Western Samoa, who voiced the same loud criticism and showed the same appalling ignorance of the countries in which they were supposed to be helping.

Next day found us up on the Nyika plateau at some 7,300 feet, in open country studded with great rocky outcrops, with hardly a tree to be seen; reminiscent in many ways of the Central Otago area in New Zealand. We saw little wildlife up there, but a surprising number of flowers nestling in the long grass and in the lee of the outcrops. There were few villages to be seen, for this was no easy area in which to live and grow crops. We spent the night in a government rest house at one of the highest points on the road, sitting talking during the evening to others staying there, and feeding a big log fire. It was the coldest night we ever experienced in Africa, but an interesting experience to have been up there and have seen a part of the territory that was so very different. Descending from the plateau on the following day, we moved briefly into Nyasaland (now Malawi), passing through Fort Hill, where we paused for lunch before moving back into Northern Rhodesia to reach Isoka. By noon on the next day we were back in Kasama, our local leave over, but with a host of memories and some excellent photographs. From that time our children's love of animals and I think our own, too, was intensified, and we are still members of the World Wildlife Fund.

It was along the Nyasaland border that one of African education's more amusing incidents occurred, before the time of our visit to that part of the world. A new, keen, young district education officer was out on tour, inspecting schools in the particular area for the first time, fired with enthusiasm. He came across a small, two-teacher school and, although the name was unfamiliar and it was not on his list, he decided to inspect it. He found it something of a shambles, told off both teachers, closed the school, and sent the children home until such time as the list of things he gave the staff to do had been dealt with. He drove off in high dudgeon, but feeling pleased that he had acted firmly and decisively. A couple of days later he arrived back at his office at district headquarters. No sooner had he arrived than a more than slightly annoyed district commissioner appeared. 'May I ask where you have been?' that gentleman enquired rather ominously. The education officer told him, adding, 'And just as well I went. That particular school was a shambles. I closed it and –'. 'I know,' snapped the district commissioner, 'but unfortunately, you bloody idiot, you closed a school in Nyasaland!' I believe the keen young education officer looked so crestfallen that the district commissioner relented and the session ended in laughter. But wires had been hot for a time and the African education department had had some careful explaining to do. When I travelled over to the eastern parts of Northern Rhodesia and actually entered Nyasaland, I could see how easy it was for this to have occurred. The road in parts runs right along the border and there is nothing to indicate in which territory you are. We did not know exactly when we moved into Nyasaland nor when we moved out again. And I can well imagine the teachers of a small rural school being too alarmed to say anything when a European education officer descended on them out of the blue, especially when he quickly became irate at what he found there. His driver probably knew they were across the border, but he, too, would have said nothing. The way of the *bwana* was often completely incomprehensible; many of them seemed to be mad anyway and one did not argue with a madman!

Looking back on our visit to the Luangwa valley, once we had returned to our more or less normal life in Kasama, I contemplated our trip and was particularly interested in the attitude of Africans to wildlife, an attitude I have thought about a lot since. It was unfortunately the advent of Europeans that brought about the poaching and large scale killing of animals, for before their arrival the Africans killed only when they needed to, generally for meat and skins. Things like ivory had a value within the tribe and were much prized, but, until they came to mean money and could be traded for goods such as guns and metal utensils, there was little wholesale killing of animals, particularly the elephant and the rhinoceros. Man and nature were more balanced; the way the wildlife has been decimated since the Arabs and the white man penetrated Africa shows where the blame lies. Africans generally have a great respect for wildlife out in the rural areas, and a great rapport with nature and the bush, although a lot of that feeling has been lost in the towns. Too many Europeans, and then too many Africans, saw wild animals as nothing more than money on four legs. Too many of them still do. Europeans quickly realised the dangers of over-hunting and, especially since independence has swept through Africa, many Africans also now see healthy, live animals as more valuable than dead ones. In the deep bush, in the small villages, it goes deeper than that, for the rural African understands the nature around him, and does not think of it as subordinate to himself. He does not try to master it, but only to live with it, at one with his environment. I think this has helped many Africans to understand the value of tourism, for many African countries, poor in soil and resources, have to look to tourism as a substantial source of income, though it has taken many of them a long time to realise this fully. I have always been struck by the way the rural African understood the wildlife. I suppose one is more likely to develop that understanding if one lives a subsistence life, growing what one eats, moving about only within a narrow tribal area. In those circumstances, one's very survival tends to depend on a deep understanding of nature in all its forms.

Animals were still to the fore when we got back to Kasama. We found Buster in great form, but Frixos, probably as the result of a bite of some kind, had a bad leg, obviously poisoned. We did things in Africa that we would not have had to do almost anywhere else, as does everyone. First we took Frixos to the hospital, where one of the doctors have him an injection to slow down the poisoning process. Then we got on to Abercorn by telephone, for that was where the vet was stationed, and arranged for him to see Frixos the next day. With all the work I had waiting for me after our short spell of leave, I could not leave the office, so next morning Hazel and Brennian set off in the car for Abercorn, a hundred and six miles away. I sent one of my messengers with them. They set off about 7.30 and were back again by the early afternoon, complete with one puss, an abscess removed from his leg, pumped full of antibiotics, but bright-eyed and hungry! Thinking about this afterwards, we wondered how many people in the 'civilised' world would have thought us mad, taking a cat to the public hospital and then driving over two hundred miles to get expert attention from the veterinary officer. But that was Africa, and no one in Kasama thought we were mad, European or African. In fact, for weeks afterwards the messenger who went as escort on that trip kept enquiring after Frixos' health.

In the meantime, I had also had quite an eventful day. I got a message, more or less a cry for help, from the Roman Catholic Fathers at Malole, quite a few miles out. The secondary school was out on strike. Knowing what could happen on such occasions, I went out there very quickly, accompanied by the manager of schools. The pupils would not go into class and would not talk to the teachers nor to the Fathers, but were sitting around, peacefully enough, many of them dozing in the shade. A talk with the Fathers elicited the fact that one of them had, in telling a boy off, called him a 'bloody fool'. My manager and I immediately guessed that this was probably the key to the whole thing. We walked out into the grounds, sat down on a big log under a tree, and beckoned the boys. No one moved for a couple of minutes and then one by one they got up to come around us, squatting on the ground in a semi-circle. We talked generally for a few minutes and then the boy whose misdemeanour had set the whole thing off came forward to squat right at my feet. 'The Father,' he said, 'he call me bloodful. What is this bloodful? Is it curse so that I go sick, maybe die?' I met my manager's eye, but we made no show of our feelings. 'No,' I told the boy, 'it is not a curse. But Mr Chellahs will explain it to you in your own language.' The manager did this, and I heard him explain in Bemba, 'It meant you were very stupid and I think you were, but you should have told the Father you did not understand.' Then he added, 'Remember this is a mission school and you are a Christian. The Fathers do not curse people like witch-doctors. But if you do not behave, you will probably go to hell!' On that note I chimed in quickly to reassure the boy that hell was still a long way off. There were satisfied murmurs all round; the boy promptly got up and led the way back to the classrooms, the whole school following, laughing and chattering. We stayed around for another hour or more, while teaching resumed, but everything went on just as if nothing had happened. We were able to come away with peace clearly restored.

Before the end of the year we had another contretemps, a more serious one this time, since it involved a female sent to us by the V.S.O. organisation, UNIP, and the Special Branch of the police. V.S.O. personnel were sent to us from time to time to help in the schools, though I could never quite decide whether they were supposed to be helping the Africans or helping themselves. They usually came straight from school before going on to university, full of enthusiasm, but which was often misplaced because their heads were full of jargon about 'colonial oppressors' and woolly ideas about noble savages, discrimination and exploitation. But they did at least know a little more about Africa than the American

Peace Corps people we encountered. The particular female we had in Kasama was young and very naive. I had already alerted the manager of schools and he in turn had some trusted headmasters on the watch. It soon became clear that the young lady was getting herself heavily involved with the local UNIP hierarchy. Late in August she threw a party at her house, inviting my wife and me, along with several other Europeans. The rest of the people were all African, and I noticed six of the top UNIP officials in the area. Thereafter the stories flew thick and fast. The girl was frequently in the African suburb late into the night and more than once showed herself rather self-consciously in the shops, handling an African baby or carrying it on her back, African style. The child was not hers, but it seemed as if she wanted to create the impression that it was. There was talk all round the township, not so much among the Europeans as among the Africans themselves. Like so many naive 'do-gooders', she did not realise that Africans wanted Europeans to be and act like Europeans, doing their job alongside them, helping them, but not trying to intrude into their lives and, above all, not intruding into their politics. UNIP was strong, but the great majority of its members did not want Europeans in their ranks.

In her complete failure to understand the situation our female V.S.O. not only caused controversy and unrest, but was actually putting her own life at risk. I conferred with the district commissioner and the Special Branch officer in Kasama, and then called the girl in for a talk. She barely listened to what was said to her, before launching into a typical harangue about her soul, Christian ideals, colonialism, and how we misunderstood the people who were running UNIP. I suffered a reasonable period of this before cutting her short and explaining what she was doing to the Africans around her, to herself, and to the department. She went off, muttering about her soul, and continued to blunder on in the same unthinking manner. A report was made to headquarters in Lusaka, which, as I expected, advised a 'do nothing for a while' policy in 'this delicate political situation'. The only thing I could do was pass the matter quietly to the provincial commissioner himself; he seemed to pull the requisite strings and in a few weeks the girl in question was gone, transferred to Lusaka. Everyone

118

around Kasama, African as well as European, breathed sighs of relief. I had always questioned the value of sending what were in effect senior school children out to places like Africa, completely inexperienced, but at the age where they thought they knew it all and nobody over forty knew anything. Occasionally we found a really worthwhile volunteer, usually a little older, better qualified, and far less naive, but in general they all needed the most careful guidance and handling. A similar service in New Zealand (the V.S.A.) presented the same problems, as I found out later in Western Samoa, but they also accepted much older and qualified people in the Pacific, in general achieving better results because of this greater maturity.

The year 1963 began well, but was marred in Kasama by the death of a small girl, the daughter of friends of ours, who was knocked down by a truck right outside her own home. Events like that affected everyone in a place the size of Kasama and almost the entire European population and hundreds of Africans turned up for the funeral. Apart from that unexpected and unhappy event, things were now developing more or less as expected. With independence scheduled for 1964, the UNIP representatives in all areas – and especially here in the Bemba stronghold – became ever louder and bolder. Britain now threw her full weight behind the break-up of the Federation, and there were also some unpleasant signs of possible twisting and turning over the colonial service terms of service and compensation. This caused unrest among European officers, particularly when officers who were outspokenly anti-UNIP began to be transferred, either right into Lusaka under the eagle eye of the top echelons, or out into some remote area where they would be virtually unheard. We in the Northern Province, right in the very heart of UNIP country, were shrewd enough to go on quietly with our jobs and to avoid, as far as possible, any clashes with UNIP officials. I must say that, for the most part, UNIP did not seem to want confrontation either, and for the next year there was an uneasy truce which at least enabled us to get on with our work and try to make sure that we advanced as far as we could before handing over the reins to our African successors. Despite this, there were one or two inevitable clashes and on these I stood firm – and because I stood firm, the party officials tended to back down.

One particular occasion was when I had a visit from a UNIP delegation of three, demanding that I remove the pictures of the Queen from my offices and from the schools. I gave them a flat 'No', and explained that they would remain until the day of independence. After that, whoever was in charge at a particular place could remove or retain the pictures as he or she wished, for the Queen would still be the Head of State – if only, perhaps, a figurehead. One of the delegation began to bluster. 'We demand their removal,' he shouted, hoping, no doubt, that every African in the office was listening. 'You can't demand anything,' I told him bluntly. 'You're a Party official here in Kasama. You've no authority over any government officer. If word comes from the government in Lusaka, then they will be removed. Until that happens, they stay.' The delegation left, oddly enough all shaking hands with me as they did so. We heard no more about pictures of the Queen, not even after independence in the six months that I remained in the new Zambia

Early in the year, the department in Kasama was faced with a high-powered visitor, a colonial office adviser, Miss Freda Gwilliam, a most forthright and impressive lady, who generally knew what she was talking about. By great good fortune I knew her from my days in Cyprus some twelve year earlier. I had escorted her round schools and institutions there and she was a person who respected on-the-spot local knowledge. She would quickly let someone know if she thought he was not right on target in his work. She duly arrived, full of energy as usual, and fully conversant with all my doings since I had left Cyprus. We travelled around as much as two days would allow, and also attended several social functions including a buffet meal at our house for all the leading figures in African education, both European and African, the provincial commissioner and the district commissioner. Her visit was a great success and she did more in a couple of days to impress on everyone that there were colonial office people who were really interested in education and progress than most such visitors could have done in weeks. Despite the good impression Miss Gwilliam made, though, she could not alter our perception of the general attitude in the United Kingdom. As we saw it in Rhodesia, their sole concern in Britain seemed to be to unload responsibility as quickly as possible, to let the new African states have their heads, and then free themselves of things like the colonial service. We were already no longer even called that; we had become Her Majesty's Overseas Civil Service, and 'colonial' had become a dirty word, even in Britain, especially to those who had never been to Africa and knew little or nothing about its people.

Fortunately there were some in Britain who fought for colonial service officers and appreciated the work they had done and were, in fact, still doing. If it had not been for such people, I am afraid the British government would have blatantly sidestepped a lot of its obligations and broken many of its promises. The main interest in Whitehall seemed to be in world opinion, which was as misinformed and as biased as that of Britain, and especially in American opinion, which was desperate to see the final demise of the British Empire. The Empire had become an anachronism – everyone accepted that – but a more dignified evolution to a Commonwealth and an association of independent states, based on British law and money and effort, could have been achieved, leaving a more influential Britain in future years. In my opinion, there was too much bowing and deferring to radical and liberal opinion; though some of this was, no doubt, hard to avoid for the politician, whose first thought, despite fine words, is always for himself, his image and his survival.

In July I experienced the first break in my family with the death of my mother back in New Zealand. I actually received the news in a manner more reminiscent of the turn of the century than the 1960s. I was out on tour in the Chinsali area and had gone out from Chinsali itself to a bush school some ten or twelve miles away. I was busy there, observing a teacher at work, when a runner arrived, sent after me by the district commissioner in Chinsali. This messenger was literally a runner, who had jogged the whole way, bearing in his belt the telegram that gave me the sad news. I had an hour or so of work still to do, but I offered him a lift back. He smiled happily, thanked me, and said he would be back in Chinsali before me; he was, of course. My mother had been ill for some time and had been in hospital for a couple of weeks, but her death still came unexpectedly and was a big blow to all the family. She died almost exactly a month before we set off on our leave to the United Kingdom, the Continent and New Zealand, so we were never able to tell her that we visited her home village, Farnley Tyas, in Yorkshire, nor could we show her the photos we took of her old home. Dad was still there in New Zealand, and the latter part of our leave was very good for him, as well as for all of us.

It was a splendid leave, despite my mother not being there when we finally reached New Zealand. We went first to England by air in a rather ponderous Britannia, landing at Entebbe and at Nice on the way, the unscheduled stop at Nice being forced by strong head winds which meant we had to refuel. After a week in London, we set off on a continental bus tour that took us to six countries, an excellent tour that concentrated on six main cities, leaving us time in each place to move around for ourselves. We all agreed that Vienna and Venice were probably the places we liked best. Apart from a minor smash in France, when a car – with five priests in it! – ran into us, everything went very well. October saw us back in England again, where we hired a car and drove ourselves over many interesting back roads, staying wherever we reached by evening: as far north as the Moray Firth and Inverness, and then back down through the Lake District, as far as Bristol and Stonehenge. We started and finished that part of our leave in Canterbury. We then spent a few more days in London before we sailed for New Zealand via the Azores, Panama, and Tahiti. Since those days, both our children have travelled and worked in various parts of the world, but I think they still remember that leave as something special.

The final days in New Zealand were a little grim, for we left the children at boarding schools in Wanganui and in Wellington, flying back to Africa this time by way of Australia, the Cocos Islands, Mauritius and South Africa. We were back in Kasama towards the end of February, knowing by that time that our days in Africa were numbered, but at least we had had time to get used to the idea. I certainly plunged straight back into work. On my second day at my office, I was called to the trades' school at Lukashya, where there was a sudden strike, politically inspired. As soon as I had found out what lay behind it, I sent a message to the local

UNIP office, asking their chairman to come out. Obviously rather surprised – and flattered – at being invited to participate, he arrived at the school in quick time and in the matter of about an hour we had settled the strike. The boys were back in class and the UNIP chairman departed with repeated assurances that his Party members would not interfere in the schools again. I must say, too, that for the rest of his time in Kasama he kept to those assurances remarkably well. It was a pity that more of the Party officials could not see reason and talk calmly the way he could. For my part, I could see that, with independence now only a few months away and UNIP the party of power, especially in the Northern Province, it was no use engaging them in endless confrontation. We had to get along with them and try to smooth the way for our teachers and those who replaced us. But this did not mean bowing down to their every wish by any means. UNIP itself began to realise that it was in their own interest to be reasonable, and the British have always been good at working out a compromise that gives them what they want, even if they have to concede something in the process. I did not realise that I, as a New Zealander, had this British talent until I was faced with situations where I had to use such diplomatic skills.

Over the previous year there had been big changes in Northern Rhodesia. With the demise of the Federation, all Federal concerns had again become territorial, so we now had one Department of Education embracing all races and all schools. Former European schools became fee-paying schools open to Africans who cared to pay the fees involved; this was, of course, a transition compromise. The minister of education, who had been an African for some years, now controlled all education, taking his advice from the Education department, which was, of course, still largely European in its senior posts. The parliamentary secretary for education, however, was a man of mixed blood, what the South Africans call a 'coloured'; in a way, perhaps, this was yet another compromise. I had just dealt with the Lukashya strike, when I got word to head for Chinsali to meet this very man, Thornicroft by name, who was making a visit to the Chinsali and Abercorn areas, in essence a political visit, organised by UNIP. As headquarters in Lusaka rightly observed, one did not let politicians loose on their own, so I had to be on the spot while he was in my domain. It meant a week of touring with him and a certain amount of fencing with local Party officials. Fortunately, the parliamentary secretary was a sensible man with at least some genuine interest in education, so he carefully steered a course that would avoid trouble with either government (in this case, me!) or UNIP. At night, the Party took care of him and for the most part I did not know exactly where he was; by day I planned for him and guided him around, and no one from the Party came with us when we visited schools. The tour went without a hitch, although I was aware of various undercurrents all the time. Thornicroft was adamant; the tour plan had been his, he declared, and I had simply organised what he had asked me to do. A quiet, rather diffident man in many ways, he was a born politician in other respects, with a talent for stopping the boat from rocking, particularly as far as I was concerned. From Abercorn he headed straight back for Lusaka in his limousine; I followed to Kasama in my Land-Rover, pleased to have what might have been a difficult week behind me. One of my great pleasures now was to return to a bright, open house with my wife there. For the moment there was no job for her in Kasama, but a vacancy was coming up in about a month.

In the final run up to independence, all sorts of problems arose at headquarters in Lusaka. The Biscuit Factory was no longer producing as much as it had done in the past, nor doing so as smoothly. Each European who left was, of course, replaced by an African, new to the job and lacking in experience. The Africans, in general, were keen to learn and get on with the job, but there was an inevitable slowing down all along the line. Early in March my European accountant departed for good, to South Africa. The news came that, for the time being, there was no replacement in prospect. Headquarters simply had no one to send to a remote place like Kasama, hundreds of miles away up north there in the bush! There is no doubt they were really stretched to find suitably qualified people, and in the accounting field the possibilities of error and corruption loomed large. It was at this stage that I was very thankful for that spell on accounts in Ndola years before. In fact, I was able to keep our accounts clerks on the rails quite successfully. The most senior of my education officers had now

124

also been transferred to Ndola, as yet without replacement, so the staffing problems were multiplying. The colonial service was clearly in its dying days in Northern Rhodesia – and generating a lot of confusion in the process. I found it was taking between forty and fifty days to send something to Lusaka and get an answer back; an answer that often indicated that my letter had not been read carefully or the point had been missed, so the whole process had to start all over again.

With many officers leaving just before, or at the time of, independence, there was a great deal of movement in all departments of the government service, with more and more Europeans being withdrawn to Lusaka to fill gaps there. One feature at this stage was the attitude of the provincial administration. Their officers, not trained in specialist fields, were looking for ways to remain in Northern Rhodesia in the service of the new government, and one bright idea that emerged – from Lusaka naturally – was that provincial administration officers no longer required as district commissioners and district officers should take over all the administrative posts in other departments. In true government style, this was propounded indirectly at first. Circulars and letters appeared, suggesting that specially qualified officers should be withdrawn to very specialist posts and, of course, education became one of the chief targets. Trained men – like myself – should be in the secondary schools and the teachers' colleges, while former P.A. officers could take over posts such as those of provincial education officer or the administrative jobs in headquarters: the top jobs in the education field! When this plan became clear, it got the reception it deserved and we heard no more of it, but it was a serious effort to find posts for former P.A. officers at our expense. It did not make for good feeling between European officers in their final months in Northern Rhodesia. In the eyes of many, the provincial administration never recovered its standing in the colonial service in Northern Rhodesia after that effort. Fortunately there was plenty of work to do, especially as we were short-handed, and that kept our minds off these incidents. However, our work was not helped by the antics of Alice Lenshina, once again in the Chinsali area.

125

Alice Lenshina was a kind of religious fanatic, who claimed she was in direct communication with God. She made all sorts of prophecies and promises, most of them naturally quite ambiguous, so that she could always claim to have been right. Hundreds of ordinary Africans flocked to Alice Lenshina, who was operating in the Chinsali district, most of them uneducated, and before long she was making subversive statements. Her followers became violent, threatening people, destroying property, beating people up, and finally killing. The police and the army had to move in. Some of my outlying primary schools were burned down by these fanatics; many more had to close for the time being. We could enter the area ourselves only with police and army permission. Lenshina and her horde were finally confronted at a place called Sioni, where in a pitched battle seventy-one of them were killed and over a hundred wounded, but she herself and her immediate disciples escaped, while the rest scattered to re-assemble later for a further confrontation. In the end, over two hundred of them were killed and an unknown number wounded before Lenshina was captured to be sent away and placed under restriction in another part of the country. Just what Lenshina wanted was never quite clear; it seemed that she sought to establish and rule her own community with her own laws and methods. Her quest was humorous, pathetic, and very dangerous all at the same time, costing a number of innocent lives and a great deal of destruction and disruption. It was also the first crisis a by now largely African government in Northern Rhodesia had to face, and they showed glimpses of the ruthlessness already evident in many independent states.

Nearer home, at my headquarters in Kasama, I had further problems. I had at long last been sent a European accountant, well qualified and good at his job. But it seemed he was just as good at other things, too, and he was soon involved with an African woman, who was calculating enough to proceed to blackmail him. Fortunately he came to me with his problems, very contrite, and terrified of his wife. With the help of my African education officer, who had also now joined me, I located the woman and had her summoned to the office along with her husband, who was in on what promised to be a lucrative scheme. We destroyed the

126

whole plan, threatened the woman and her husband with the police, sent them back to work, and then made the accountant confess all to his wife to clear away any possibility of further blackmail. It turned out, unfortunately for the accountant, that his wife had strong feelings about fidelity, and she insisted that the wretched man must publicly grovel and confess his sins to the world, after which he would be allowed to remain in their house. After a suitable period of repentance they would 'remarry' and start afresh, with herself very much the mistress of the house and family. I was able to talk her out of the public performances, but later they actually did go through a ceremony of 'remarriage', even though there had been no divorce nor even separation. If they had lived in the eighteenth century, she would very probably have had him in the pillory and branded with a hot iron.

Soon after, our provincial commissioner retired and returned to Scotland, leaving us mourning the loss of a good man who had gained the respect and confidence of all officers, regardless of their department. He was replaced by a new phenomenon – the Resident Under Minister – an African substitute for the provincial commissioner and a purely political appointment: no qualifications, no training, only long and faithful service to UNIP. By great good fortune he had enough sense to leave most of the provincial heads of departments alone to get on with their jobs; he may well have been advised to do so. He was an uncommunicative, stony-faced man, seemingly completely controlled by Party officials. He was ill at ease with Europeans and clearly did not like them, but he had that one saving grace – he left us alone. One by one European officers were departing, to be replaced by Africans, or not to be replaced at all. The government was slowing down perceptibly, but at least it was still functioning, despite all the delays and the frustrations.

Within the family we had our problems also. Rosalind, unlike her brother, was quite unable to settle and fit into boarding school life, so, after a term of frustrations and distress and disappointment, we brought her back to Africa, right up to Kasama, to live at home and do her school work by correspondence. That did not have the effect on her work that we feared it might, because the fact that she was happy and much more relaxed meant that she worked very well.

Brennian, always the more gregarious of the two, was not troubled at all and spent five years at boarding school, for the last year of which we were back in New Zealand, after three years in Western Samoa. Like most other European officers, in 1964 I began the search for jobs away from Africa, for I could see that staying in the new independent territory would not suit me, especially as political interference was beginning to become evident right at the top in Lusaka. Before the end of the year I had offers of two good jobs, one as a university lecturer, and one as the assistant director of education in Western Samoa; I chose the latter and within a few months of my arrival in Samoa in 1965 I had become the director, a post which I held until my contract there expired at the end of 1967. The decision in 1964 took a lot of thought, but we never regretted the choice of Samoa and spent a very pleasant and interesting three years there.

Western Samoa was a great contrast to Africa and especially to that part of Africa that we had grown to know so well. It consisted of two reasonably large, and numerous small, islands. It was sharply rugged, very humid and tropical. The seasons were not as clearly defined as they were in Africa, and the temperature varied less. The close presence of the sea, the coral reefs, the rapid, lush growth, the easy manner of the people: all these things struck us immediately. Most Samoans spoke quite good English, and all had a fairly close affinity with New Zealand; many had been educated there. In fact, some thirty thousand Samoans live in Auckland alone, many of them born there. In Samoa there is no harshness about life as there is in parts of Africa. In many ways its people are more sophisticated than the Africans south of the Sahara, but they do not generally have quite as close a link with their land; though the older they were, the greater was their bond with their land and the nature around them. The great ambition of most young Samoans was, and still is, to get away to work in New Zealand, or sometimes Australia, and settle there. Most Africans we knew loved best the peace and quiet of their own villages and tribal lands; most Samoans wanted the bustle and excitement of a city like Auckland. I was always glad I went to Samoa after my years in Africa. I think, because of that, I understood both the Africans and the Samoans better. But, although Samoa was a very pleasant and interesting place, it never cast a spell on me in the way that Africa did. It is to that bewitching continent that we must now return.

Independence came remarkably quietly in October 1964, without the violence that some had predicted. In Kasama, typical ceremonies and celebrations were held. On the evening before, the union jacks came down at all government offices for the last time. I took a photo of it happening at our office and I still have the flag that came down. Next morning, the new Zambian flag went up for the first time and I took a photo of that also. Technically, we moved into our final six months in Africa as aliens in a foreign land, officers on loan to the new government, with the option of taking out a new contract when those six months came to an end. Not many did in the education field, for the choice of job was very restricted and no advancement was possible for contract officers. In November my 'shadow' arrived, an African education officer, a good one, whom I had known for years, first as a headmaster, and then as a manager of schools. We got on well because we knew each other's working habits already and we seemed to complement each other. I knew the province would be in good hands when I left and it made those last months more pleasant than they might have been. My successor possessed a rare and subtle sense of humour.

Once Zambia had come into existence, the pace of departures quickened and friends of many years disappeared, moving to Rhodesia (which was still a long way from becoming Zimbabwe), to South Africa, or back to the United Kingdom. It seemed as if every European in Zambia was on the move, either back to the bigger centres or out of the country. A few of us remained to carry on in the outlying stations like Kasama and I think we were, in many respects, better off than those who were moved into the large towns or were already stationed there. Rural Africa did not change much and, apart from a few UNIP officials who were sent out from the towns to agitate in the countryside regions, independence brought little immediate change to our daily lives or work. We felt no sense of danger. There was little noticeable change of attitude, except perhaps some slackening of effort on the part of our clerks and messengers. In some cases they obviously felt there was no longer the same need to follow the standards set by the European officers.

Our final months, the first few of 1965, passed quickly because we were all kept busy. I had one visit from the new minister of education, a former secondary school teacher, who did not like Europeans and made no secret of the fact. The visit went by well enough, although it was all rather stiff and formal. Even my African 'shadow' remarked that he was 'a cold fish' who had made little attempt to be friendly or relaxed with anyone, even the African staff. In March I flew out of Africa for good, called urgently to Western Samoa; so urgently, in fact, that my wife and daughter had to follow a fortnight later on our original bookings. My departure was quiet, without much celebration or fuss, because most of our friends had already gone, though a few remained for some months after us. Up there in Kasama there were many Africans who were sad to see us go and who let us know that in a quiet way. I felt, though, that with the political guardians watching them and their minds on the future, they dare not show too much feeling. My replacement, the new provincial education officer, the African I had known for a great deal of my time in the country, showed more emotion than any other African I knew. As I flew south to Johannesburg on a beautiful, clear day, I was able to watch the Zambesi pass beneath me – and I was gone from Northern Rhodesia after more than eleven years. I can still see the silver line of the river, and the green and brown and red of the land. I remembered once taking a drink from the river, as we ran smoothly along with the current out in midstream, the paddlers at rest. My *kapitao*, the barge master, had smiled and said, 'Bwana, you drink the waters. One day you will be back, maybe two years, maybe twenty years, but you will be back!' So far it has not happened – but, who knows?

7

Impressions

More than a decade in Africa was bound to leave a lasting impression and overall it is a good one. I do not flatter myself that I made much impression as an individual, but the colonial service as a whole, and I was a part of it, certainly did. But for the individual the real impression comes the other way; it is Africa that encroaches on his senses, his feelings. He goes there, he meets it, and its land and its people draw him in. One does not conquer Africa; one becomes to some degree a part of it and that part remains always, for the rest of one's life. This thing, this feeling, this Africa, transcends politics and the struggle of man to achieve something, for man is really quite insignificant. Africa, one could say, is timeless and unconquerable, but man is neither.

I feel that Africans, no matter where they are in the continent, are basically simple people. 'Civilisation', as understood by Europeans, and sophistication are a veneer. Underneath that veneer there is still the simple subsistence dweller. At the same time there is shrewdness, because the African can calculate and often get what he wants by agreeing (or at least appearing to agree) with you. The villager may be ignorant of the world beyond his own village or beyond his tribal area, but he is far from stupid. It could be said that, when a man goes to Africa to live and work there, he spends his first three years getting to know the people and realising that they are not all the same, any more than Europeans are. His next three years he spends learning how Africans think, and how to put himself into their way of thinking when the occasion demands. In his

131

next three years and beyond he begins to understand them and with that to realise just how much he still does not know about them. To my mind no one can begin to understand the African until he has been there for at least five or six years. I am often amused – and frequently irritated - by the way we are bombarded by the pronouncements of 'experts' who have read a lot about Africa and spent three weeks there 'to get some local colour'. Three *years* is not enough to reach a decent understanding.

The feelings are mutual, of course. Africans do not understand us any more quickly or fully than we understand them. Gradually they learn to do so, but often, in the process, they try to become European in outlook and lose touch with a great deal of the basic philosophy of their people. Centuries ago, Europeans had the equivalent of tribal affinities. Africans still have these today, and very strongly. They are something we often find hard to understand, but, for example, an African regards it as only natural that, once in a position of power and influence, he should give to relatives and members of his own tribe any lesser positions that are at his command. We still do the same thing to some degree, but now usually in the commercial and the business world. Overall I feel that one can get along with Africans, if one makes the effort to understand them and their feelings. But, if one is the man in charge, one must show firmness, for Africans despise weakness in any form in a leader. At the same time, of course, though, one must listen and respect their points of view. Thankfully, Westerners no longer think of Africans as some sort of talking animal, but nor are Africans just like us except in colour of skin. Far too many Europeans fail to grasp this. Of course, Africans are just as likely as us to be intelligent, moral, honest and hard-working (or devious, criminal and power-hungry), but the differences between us in culture and outlook can be enormous.

One respect in which there is a big difference is in thinking and beliefs. African religion is close to nature, not an abstract thing in the mind, or a philosophy of idealism, as it is for many Europeans. The spiritual world is very real to most Africans, and for this reason witchcraft has a hold and a reality that we cannot quite grasp. It seems to produce situations and events that often do not seem possible; what has happened is either true and real, or there has been an incredible series of coincidences. I commented earlier that no one who has been in Africa for any length of time scoffs at witchcraft and dismisses it out of hand. To begin with, it is real to the African and can have a deep psychological effect on him. Witch-doctors are important people in the community, regularly consulted as we consult a doctor or perhaps a priest, for the witch-doctor is both. He often makes use of good, effective, natural remedies for physical ailments. His power is, however, based on fear, the fear the community has of him. I saw this in action more than once and heard of many other instances, even including ritual murder.

Witch-doctors used traditional objects: bones; masks; wooden dolls, some benign, some incredibly evil in expression. On one occasion I was involved with the district commissioner in organising a gathering of Africans prominent in the local community for a sort of seminar on witchcraft in an effort to counteract some of its influence. We got most of the top teachers from the area along and for a couple of days the subject was discussed, opinions asked, opinions given, suggestions made. The teachers, men well educated and experienced in a remote community such as this was, all contributed sensible comment and agreed that the bad aspects of witchcraft must be counteracted. For the final session, the district commissioner himself brought along a basket full of bones, small wooden dolls, hair, teeth, all things found by the police over the past year and confiscated. He spoke about them. The teachers agreed that things such as this could have no real power. They nodded sagely to one another. Then the D.C. lifted a wooden doll from the basket. 'Here,' he said to one of my prominent and respected head teachers sitting in the front row, 'feel that thing and have a good look at it.' The teacher leapt clean over the back of his chair. The man beside him leapt sideways on top of those next to him. Not one of the more than twenty people present would touch that doll or anything else from the basket. And yet in experience and knowledge of the wider world all these men were far ahead of the average villager. The D.C. handled the situation well, with no sign of annoyance or superiority, nor did he make any attempt to put pressure on those present. Their faces told us how they all felt inside.

Another incident that directly concerned me was the case of a clerk in the office, who became very quiet, listless, and apparently uninterested in his work, so I got my senior African clerk and head messenger to do some detective work for me. It seemed that the young clerk had fallen foul of the uncle of the girl he was hoping to marry. The bones had been pointed, to many Africans virtually a death sentence. I tried to make arrangements to move the clerk to another area, but it was too late. The psychological power of the witch-doctor, or the evil spirit he had released, whichever way one looked at it, had already taken a firm hold. The young man died in just three weeks, gradually sinking into lethargy, ceasing to move from his hut, eating nothing, wasting away until he passed into a sort of coma and died. Our European doctor could do nothing; the young man, it seemed, had made up his mind that he must die – and he did.

Both these happenings can be explained away by psychology, as I well knew – and was told very loftily by a young, know-all university lecturer back in New Zealand much later. Needless to say he had never been to Africa. The same explanation could apply to one of my own house servants, who literally went mad and had to be taken away to a mental hospital. According to my cook, a witch-doctor had put the finger on him, but I never found out further details in his case. Witchcraft is a powerful force in African society; once experienced, as I experienced it, it becomes very real and is never forgotten. Some things cannot be explained, but in most such cases the evidence is largely hearsay or could possibly be coincidental. Very little in witchcraft is ever clear cut, but most witch-doctors had an aura of mystery, a sort of spirituality. Some had a very distinct aura of evil, which even Europeans could often feel. I met two witch-doctors in my time in Africa, and one of them had that aura which made me feel cold even in the heat of the tropics.

Perhaps the strongest impressions for me, the most lasting ones, come from the land itself. Its sheer size makes man insignificant. From our days in Northern Rhodesia I remember most vividly those occasions out in the bush when I paused to think just how far I was from the nearest settlement, or I looked at the Zambesi in flood across the Barotse plain when water stretched for more than twenty miles. In Africa, one never felt that man had control of the situation, not even in the areas that were settled and supposedly civilised. Everything happened on a big scale. Africa stirred itself every now and then and threw that parasite, man, off its back, but then, perhaps like a sated lion, it went back to sleep, allowing man to crawl around again until it once more became irritated and threw him aside for a while. Even though it was never really cold in the Africa we knew, there were seasonal changes in the land and the plant life. We were always struck by the fact that a great deal of the new growth on trees and shrubs was red, so that the equivalent of spring often looked more like our autumn. In the dry season vast areas looked virtually dead, almost like a desert, until the first rain fell. Everything then came to life almost overnight and there was rapid growth, not lush like that in the Pacific, but steady and heavy right through the wet season. Bush fires often occurred, but they burned comparatively slowly, unlike those in Australia, where a man can get caught and trapped in a matter of minutes. In Northern Rhodesia one could outrun and easily outdrive most bush fires; nevertheless, they often burned for days. The wildlife – and, of course, the rural Africans – understood the bush very well. Animals like the various types of buck knew that fire meant new, green, sweet grass afterwards and, as the fire passed on and the ground cooled, they would converge on these areas. Most fires occurred at the end of the dry season, when the rain was near, and the first downpour was enough to set the shoots springing up, wonderful food for the close-cropping buck, the puku, the impala, and even the much larger and heavier eland.

The most striking natural phenomenon was the storm. Thunder and lightning in Africa is really something to behold. In New Zealand and the United Kingdom, a few peals of thunder constitute a thunderstorm; it is high above and often miles away. In Africa it is there, sitting right over you, and great streaks of forked lightning zigzag their way across the sky, sometimes actually striking the ground within sight. It if is also raining heavily, the lightning becomes an eerie, purple light all around you, reflected on the rain, flashing almost constantly. Anyone driving a car in a storm simply has to pull in to the side and stop. Windscreen wipers are useless and, in any case, the driver cannot see more than a few feet ahead. The thunder can be really deafening and it shakes the ground under one's feet. The clouds seem to touch the treetops; the blackest skies I have ever seen were in Africa, although those in the Pacific islands can come very close. Recently, we seem to be experiencing more violent storms in New Zealand and downpours that can flood a road in a few minutes, but even they have yet to reach the tropical level. On one occasion, miles out on a narrow and rough bush road in Northern Rhodesia, I was crossing a swamp on a causeway in the middle of a storm. The rain was not the blinding kind, so I could see for some distance. Half way across the causeway there was a bang that rattled our Land-Rover, and at the same time I saw a streak of lightning hit the swampy ground about a hundred yards to our left. My driver uttered a loud 'Sa!' as the vehicle bounced at the impact. Seconds later there was another tremendous flash, another bang, and I saw the same thing to our right, this time much closer. My driver shouted 'Awe! Jesus!' and put his foot down to get us out of that swamp fast. Fortunately we stayed on the slippery road. The next flash was further off, the rain became heavier, we slowed down to a safer speed, and both of us breathed more easily again. Dry thunderstorms, which usually occur just at the beginning of the wet season, are sometimes more frightening, because they seem more unpredictable and, with everything very dry one strike of lightning can spark off a fire. I always preferred a wet storm. Africans used to walk out in storms, and in the Copperbelt area, an average of eight to ten people a year were killed by lightning out in the open.

Rivers dominate the land and the way of life in Northern Rhodesia; firstly the Zambesi itself, and then other almost equally large ones, like the Luangwa and the Kafue. For centuries they have been lifelines sustaining the people and the wildlife, and providing a means of communication. They still do. Their flooding and receding each year make a lot of land usable for crops; few places in Northern Rhodesia are really short of water, though it is sometimes not easy to get the water where it is most needed. Rapids and falls, however, restrict communication, but very long stretches can be used in the wet season. In some places one can take a boat over what, in the dry season, is a minor waterfall. Most Africans do not tempt fate by shooting rapids; their canoes are too shallow for that and demand delicate balance, even in smooth water. As with most things in Africa, it is the size and the terrifying power of the rivers that are striking. One simply stares at them, in awe.

Many other impressions of our African days remain with us and remain for all time, but they are the personal ones, the things that happened to each of us at different times – little, unusual things. I can speak only of my own, although my wife and children also have their personal memories which I cannot relate. I find mine by looking over the pages of my diary, where every now and then some comment catches my eye, such as the fact, for instance, that on his third birthday our son celebrated by biting his sister! Fortunately, she never held it against him. The following year Brennian experimented by shutting or trying to shut Frixos in a drawer. Frixos tolerated a lot, but this was a little too much to take; he bit, and caught Brennian's cheek, whereupon there was a little panic all round and a dash to the hospital. But Brennian in his turn never held that against Frixos, though I noticed that he never again tried to push the cat into any drawers. Much later, in fact in the year we left Africa, Rosalind, by then fifteen, was sitting in our Kasama garden with her back against a low brick wall, reading. A movement caught her eye and she glanced to the right – to look more or less eyeball to eyeball at a cobra about four or five feet away! Somehow in one movement she shot from her nearly prone position into the middle of the lawn many feet away. The cobra was so startled it took off fast in the opposite direction for the bush. I heard Rosalind call out and dashed out to find her trying to work out just how she had managed to reach where she was in one bound. We could not find the snake, but its tracks were there – and Rosalind's heel marks, just one set of them!

On another occasion we went on a local leave to Lake Tanganyika to a fishing village and rest house at Sumbu. While there, the children swam in the lake and, when Brennian emerged, he was horrified and very alarmed to find a leech attached to his thigh, already swollen with blood. Leeches do not cause pain when they are attached, unless one tries to pull them off. Fortunately Brennian came to us without touching it and, thanks to my war days in the Solomon Islands jungle, I knew about leeches. I sat him down, got the salt, gave the leech a liberal dose all over, and in about a minute it was off him, shrivelling up. Brennian was left much relieved, with no more than a tiny spot of blood on his leg (whereas, if leeches are pulled off, they leave the proboscis in and a festering sore develops). In the jungle we did not usually have salt handy, so we used to burn them off us with cigarettes; which was just as effective.

Northern Rhodesia, like many other African territories, was noted for its European characters, especially in the early days: men like Codrington, whom I have already mentioned, and Chirupula Stephenson, who also played a prominent part in the country's development. I had the good fortune to meet and get to know quite well one such man, Arthur Harrington, one of two brothers who figured in Northern Rhodesia's history. Chiana was the elder brother by a considerable margin, but he died in 1941, well before my time; so I only knew him by reputation. Arthur, on the other hand, I first met in 1957, and then knew for the whole time we lived and worked in Barotseland. He lived at Senanga on the main route up and down the river, and was already aged eighty-four by then, but he remained an active and vigorous man with a fat, cheerful African wife and seemingly innumerable children aged from about thirty downwards. He knew whenever any European officer passed through Senanga, and woe betide any man who failed to call on him, even if only for a few minutes! I had a number of very interesting sessions with him. He was born in England and began his working life in an architect's office, but the urge to get away and travel was too strong. He joined the Cape mounted police in 1897 and became a quartermaster sergeant during the Boer War. After the war he moved to Southern Rhodesia and eventually, in 1907, he found his way into Northern Rhodesia, by which time he had worked as a barman, a blacksmith, a bricklayer, a carpenter, and a rigger in a gold mine. He used to tell the story of how Codrington, the administrator, offered him the post of director of public works – if he could stay sober for a fortnight. He did not succeed! Arthur moved all round Barotseland, settling in Senanga in 1935, and remaining there for the rest of his life. I used to have lively arguments – over whisky in his case and brandy in mine – about the education of African girls. Harrington, whose African name was Matepeta, did not believe they should be educated at all because 'the little bitches ought to be out looking after the village gardens'. He felt it was bad enough educating white women, but educating African girls made no sense at all! On two or three occasions he came up to Mongu and once I met him in the club there. As we sat down to a drink, he looked round the bar and asked 'Where's that young bugger Balme today?' Frank Balme was a well-known identity round Mongu, a man of long standing there; he was seventy-six! Arthur (Matepeta) Harrington died after we had left Mongu; I was always glad that I met such a character. The major activity of his Senanga days was building boats, at which he was an expert. In fact, he was responsible for the royal barges of the paramount chief and he taught many Africans some of his skills. His coloured son, Willie Harrington, carried on boat-building after his death.

I could go on recording impressions nearly indefinitely. Thinking of one incident leads me on to another, and another, and yet another. But I have resisted the temptation to keep adding to this chapter. Enough has been written to show how lasting an impression Africa makes upon people. One could not remove the mark of Africa even if one wanted to; it is indelible.

8

Vignettes

A
ccording to my dictionary, a vignette is (amongst other, wider meanings) 'a literary sketch or a character sketch'. I think the following four pieces qualify under this heading and all are very relevant to this account of our time in Africa. As I explained in an earlier section, the first, 'That Education Officer', was supposed to appear in print in the United Kingdom, but I was never able to find out whether it actually did. The second appeared in *Corona*. The two short stories were read over the air in 1962 by the Central African Broadcasting Service. I had two other stories also read on the air, but they did not deal specifically with Africa, so they are not included here. Both of the two stories are based on actual events. The basic tale of 'A Matter of Psychology' was related to me by a district commissioner of long experience, who knew a lot about African witchcraft and its deep influence and power among Africans. The story of 'The Leopardess' was told to me by an African villager, the father of a teacher, who came to visit me on behalf of his son. He spoke remarkably good English, and I found he had, in fact, worked on the mines in South Africa for a number of years.

I think these four pieces all help to add to the picture of Africa. They certainly do for me and for my wife and family.

That Education Officer
Does it say what it means or mean what it says? A ticklish problem and probably the answer is neither. As to the first point, it means a great deal more than it says, as every newly-appointed education officer soon finds out. As to the second, well, if you

stretch the meaning wide enough, perhaps it does, but it is a long stretch.

One should not join the exalted ranks of the eduction officers with any false ideas. Far too many do. Frequently the young man, glowing with pride in his newly achieved degree, fired with high thoughts of the great cause of education, enters the company of the Overseas Service, a brand new – we might almost say well-scrubbed – education officer. What visions he sees! A kind of professional den, with telephones, perhaps even a nice little secretary, himself bristling with the latest educational psychology and thinking in dignified profundity before he pronounces what shall be done. Then he lands in the middle of Africa.

A month later he frenziedly reads circular minute AB/108/CJ/2/5 for the ninth time and still cannot understand it. Then he dashes out to Yaba school to see whether the working party has dug that latrine in the right place. They haven't. So he moves on to Impanga to see how many desks need repairing and who broke the window in the headmaster's office. Education? Of course – for both the African and the European!

The great thing about education officers is that they rarely give up. The splendid visions fade, psychology becomes mere common sense, and the classical degree is exercised upon how many sheets of iron it takes to roof a building sixty feet by twenty. He works it out. He orders the iron. Then they ask him how many purlins he wants. Blast it, what *are* purlins? He thumbs the dictionary. Good God, pieces of timber to hold up the roof! He had, of course, quite forgotten that these roofs have to be supported. And so it goes on.

That is perhaps the first impression. Buildings, repairs, pay for the staff, innumerable circulars to study, and even more innumerable returns to make. But, as I say, the education officer rarely gives up and presently – perhaps after six months – the light begins to filter through. There *is* education in all of this and some progress is being made towards lifting the African to a higher level.

In general, the African responds; in his own way and in his own time, of course, but he certainly responds. Perhaps the first thing to get into the mind is that the African frequently says, not what

141

he really means, but what he thinks you want him to say. This is inclined to be infuriating, because ten minutes later he cannot remember what he said at first and the truth may even slip out. The truth can, as a rule, eventually be arrived at, but the process is often long and the road tortuous.

In other ways the African is terrifyingly logical.

'Kasembe, you haven't seen Bwana Smith, have you?'

'Yes, sir.'

'Oh, good. Where is he?'

'No, sir.'

'What?'

'Yes, sir.'

'Now look here, Kasembe, have you or have you not seen Bwana Smith?'

'Yes, sir.'

'Right. Well, where is he?'

'I don't know, sir.'

'What the devil do you mean? You just said . . .'

And so it goes on. If you think it out, the African is, in this matter, more logical than we are. He is very, very literal.

Africa is a big country and it has a lot of people. They speak a lot of languages and the new education officer laboriously learns the rudiments of one, only to find himself transferred to another district where they speak another dialect. By that time, however, he usually just shrugs his shoulders and carries on. The hardest thing in learning a language is to get the African to talk to you so that you can understand him. If you try out your Cibemba on a clerk, he listens politely and answers you in English, completely confounded as to why the *bwana* talks this appalling kind of Bemba when he, the clerk, can understand English perfectly. If you try it out on a villager, he smiles broadly and promptly pours out such a torrent of words that you cannot make head or tail of what he is saying. Meanwhile the crowd gathers to gaze on the *bwana* who can speak their own tongue. The baffled *bwana* usually retires hurriedly before the shallowness of his command of the language is disclosed. But the day comes eventually when he does not retreat hurriedly; he stops and talks – in Cibemba or whatever it happens to be – and another hurdle has been cleared.

This business of clearing the hurdles takes time and a great deal of patience. Africa in many respects still moves at the pace it did five hundred years ago. The modern features rest somewhat precariously on the surface and only gradually are their roots being put down firmly. Education is a constant battle against 'slipping back'. The African is adept at slipping back, chiefly because, generally speaking, he still likes it. Why brush the village schoolroom floor? It is only going to get just as dirty again tomorrow. Why not help the poor, dull boy in his examinations? 'Awe! He'll fail, if I don't!' The gallant education officer sets his face grimly against this, retiring out of sight from time to time either to tear his hair out or to roar with uncontrollable laughter, according to the length of time he has been in the country. Generally speaking, the longer he has been there, the louder he laughs, though there are cases of an opposite nature.

The big thing is not to let yourself be weighed down under it all, for the education officer must always face the workings of the African mind, which are, to say the least of it, somewhat peculiar to Europeans.

A teacher has been transferred and rushes in to protest.

'Bwana, it is impossible. My wife will die.'

'She will? What's the matter with her?'

'Very bad, bwana, very bad. She has not leprosy, but ringworm!'

'Hmm. And what has that to do with your transfer?'

'She cannot go. She cannot get the treatment. She will die.'

'Has she been to the hospital? Has she attended the clinic?'

'Many times, many times, but no good. Hospital is useless. Clinic is not good.'

'Indeed.'

'Now my doctor attends her.'

'Your doctor?'

'African doctor, very good.'

'Is he qualified?'

'Well, no, but . . .'

'How long did she attend the clinic?'

'Oh, much, much.'

'How long?'

'Oh, many times.'

143

'How long?'

'Three times, but . . .'

'And the hospital?'

'Much, much.'

'How many times?'

'Once, bwana, but . . .'

'When?'

'A little time ago.'

'When?'

'Very little time.'

'When?'

'Before two years, bwana.'

'And now she attends the witchdoctor, eh?'

'Yes, yes – but he is very good!'

The exasperated education officer at this stage grinds his teeth and points to the door.

'But, bwana, my wife will die! Awe, awe!'

Firmness is the only answer.

Through all this mass of contradiction, disillusionment, frustration, the education officer must battle – some say blunder – but he does and by the end of his first tour he is beginning to know what African education is all about. Circular minute AB/108/CJ/2/5 still does not make any sense, but at least he can frame an appropriate answer in flowing language. He knows about iron and purlins. He knows a great deal about latrines. He even allows a few visions to creep back in again and he has discovered that educational psychology and common sense have remarkable similarities.

So we come back to where we started and ask again what this term 'education officer' really means. He must, of course, have the academic background, but that remains only a background. What he needs most is plenty of practical common sense, a lot of energy, and a good sense of humour. His work lies in education by energy, interest, and example, and when these things are appreciated in him by the Africans, then what he says is noted and followed. It is not perhaps education as he pictured it in his dreams, when he had just applied to enter the service, but it is education, African education, and work that needs a lot of doing by the man who has to make himself a student, a teacher, an accountant, and even a builder, all rolled into one – that education officer. And he usually manages to do it.

Rhodesia Road

My driver turned to grin at me and gave a shrug.

'No road,' he said, amiably.

As the road we were on now came to a sudden end, I was forced to agree. We had run right through Luanshya and sat in our truck, perched on a hill well beyond even the second shaft of the mine. I clambered down to survey the situation, leaving my driver and orderly gabbling happily, while they waited to see what I would do.

'There must be a road further back,' I said firmly. 'Come on, get moving.'

Eventually, of course, we found it, a sandy track so mixed up with disused railway sleepers and a dilapidated iron shed that it was the easiest thing in the world to miss. But at any rate we were at last on the road to Mpongwe, weaving for the first mile or so through power pylons across cleared land. We climbed the long hill and were able to look back across the whole mine and the township before we plunged down again into thicker country.

Bush roads are intriguing. In the first place, you never know where they will turn next – contours often don't mean a thing. Secondly, I believe that Northern Rhodesia is well on the way to the discovery of the bottomless hole. These holes are invariably concealed by water. You edge your vehicle gently through and settle – equally gently – into a mass of soft, light brown liquid glue. Alternatively you decide to take things boldly and, with engine roaring, plunge through the water. A broken spring is usually the result. However, we knew what to expect and preferred the slither and slide method. It is slower, but very much safer. One usually gets there in the end. On we rolled, under a moderately cloudy sky with ever thickening bush around us.

At the Kafulafuta we stopped to study the state of the bridge and the height of the river before we ventured out over the bouncing, rattling log structure that lets things across the deep, swift river. Once across, my driver remarked that the bridge wasn't safe any more. We chugged on, lurching, bouncing, and sweeping down grass six or eight feet high in front of us every so often.

As the miles slipped gradually behind us, the sky darkened, but the rain was still well ahead. The scenery changed little – trees, puddles, high grass, thousands of butterflies, a few monkeys, an occasional villager on a bicycle, more trees. Voices came to us from time to time from the villages just off the road, and now and again small children ran, screaming excitedly, after the truck.

At length we reached a higher, drier section of track and could speed along as fast as a faulty plug would permit us. I asked my driver about spare plugs. Proudly he showed me one.

'Well, damn it, let's stop and put it in,' I said.

'No plug tool,' he said happily, and we rumbled on.

A mile or two further and we swung round a corner to come upon a remarkable scene. The track was strewn with sacks of mealie-meal, boxes of unknown content, bales of what looked like bark, oil lamps, tins of paraffin, and many smaller items. These were all placed at the side of the road in reasonably neat heaps. Two Africans sat contemplating the bush. A third casually thumbed at us along the road. We stopped; then we saw.

A well-seasoned truck stood astride a tree stump about ten yards off the road in the bush to the right.

'Truck just went into the bush and hit that tree,' explained the thumber. I eyed the curve.

'What speed were you going?' I asked.

He shrugged.

'Don't know, bwana, maybe forty,' he said, chewing grass.

Examination showed that the tree had snapped off short and lay under the front of the truck. It could be dug out.

'Spade?' I asked.

The three men just shrugged. Fortunately we had one, so we dug out the trunk and examined the vehicle. The front axle was bent and the wheels pointed gracefully inwards. My driver tried the starter and the engine let out a roar. We all heaved and pushed and cleared the stump of the tree. Then amid howls of laughter the truck moved back on to the road in a series of short bounds. By pushing desperately against one side we got it round parallel with the road and safely at one side of it. I asked if any of the men wanted to come on with us. We set off again with one of them, but only went two hundred yards before our passenger banged on the top of the cab and jumped out as the truck stopped.

'What's the trouble?' I asked.

'He wants to go the other way,' said my orderly.

We all three burst into such a roar of laughter that my driver let in the clutch suddenly and we bounced madly through three holes before he could stop. Our ex-passenger was left pointedly examining his feet, while we went on our way towards the now massive clouds.

Presently my driver nodded ahead.

'Mission,' he said.

I could not see anything but trees and long grass. We bounced through a hole and dropped steeply to a narrow bridge. One side of it hung drunkenly in four feet of water and we all climbed out to examine the situation. It did not look very good.

After a period of contemplation my driver nodded and said: 'This side good. We can get across.' I eyed him. I eyed the bridge. Then I thought of Mpongwe just ahead – on the other side. And the storm clouds hung heavy just above us.

'All right,' I said, 'here goes.'

My orderly and I walked across and stood on the other side to see what happened. The truck roared, gathered speed, and bounced crazily on to the bridge. There were two loud cracks and the structure swung up and down as if sprung. Then my driver proudly drew up alongside us, while the bridge sank gently into the water. I wiped my brow and climbed in. Chugging lustily we moved on up the hill and round a corner. On a post was a neat notice. It read 'MPONGWE MISSION'. I sighed with relief; my companions broke into high speed conversation. There was a flash of lightning and it began to rain. But we were there.

(This article was published in 1956 and I was interested to see the editor's footnote. It read: 'We were attracted by a certain agelessness in this article. We can hear old stagers from all over the colonies snorting that they went through this sort of thing twenty years or more ago. Will there still be places about which an identical article can be written in 1976? – Ed.')

A Matter of Psychology

'It's all a matter of psychology,' said the cadet, 'auto-suggestion and all that sort of stuff.'

The district commissioner took his pipe out of his mouth and blew out a cloud of smoke, watching it drift lazily round his head and finally disperse across the verandah.

'That's what they say,' he said, quietly.

'People just have to be educated up to our modern thinking,' the young man went on, 'it's just a case of eliminating the last of these old beliefs and superstitions. Anyone who thinks can see that it's all nonsense.'

'Yes,' said the D.C. drily, 'that's all.'

The cadet's flow of conversation hesitated and then stopped. He looked at his senior with a slight frown. He's been here too long, he thought, and he hasn't kept pace with things. They say these chaps can live in Africa too long. The D.C. was not looking at him, but quietly watching another cloud of tobacco smoke drift away into nothingness.

'You – you don't believe this stuff – this witchcraft stuff, do you?' the cadet asked suddenly.

The older man smiled and his clear eyes turned on the other.

'I've been in this country twenty years,' he replied, 'and I don't know.'

'But it can't be true – it – surely – '

The cadet gestured helplessly.

'That's what I used to think,' was the reply. 'Now I don't know. A lot of queer things go on in these places. Maybe it is all psychological. But I say – I don't know.'

He pointed towards the low table beside them.

'Have another drink.'

'Thanks.'

The D.C. watched him as he poured a fair measure of whisky. He noticed the young man's hand was not quite steady and that he still frowned as he added the water. He's worried, he thought, worried because this is something his degree in economics didn't teach him and never will. He's afraid, too, because he can't understand it; it doesn't fit into any pattern he knows. He lifted his own glass and took a long drink.

148

'Take this clerk chap,' he said, when the cadet sat back again. 'He's a sick man.'

'He's worried and afraid because he doesn't realise it's all just suggestion,' put in the other hurriedly.

'He's a sick man,' repeated the D.C. 'He says he's bewitched and as far as he's concerned that's that. I'm afraid it's got such a hold on him, he's going to die.'

'Impossible! There's nothing wrong with him but worry.'

'Worry can kill people, but this is more than worry. He's a sick man.'

The cadet shook his head slowly and did not speak for a while. The D.C. believes all this, he told himself, he believes this man really is bewitched. This sort of thing needs firm action and clear thinking and all he does is sit here and contemplate.

'What's going to be done?' he asked, quite sharply.

The D.C. gave him a long look.

'There's only one thing to do. Get at the root of it. Find out who's putting a spell on him and how bad the spell is.'

'Good God!'

The older man smiled.

'What else do you suggest?'

The cadet took a gulp of his drink and stared out into the night for a few moments.

'Well – er – well – I think he must just be told to shake himself out of it and get on with his job. He must pull himself together.'

The other shook his head slowly.

'It won't do,' he said quietly, 'you'll never convince him of anything like that. It's not just one man. They all believe it.'

The cadet stared at him and almost added, 'And you, too!'

Footsteps sounded along the brick path that led to the house. A figure approached rapidly, came into the light of the pressure lamp, halted with military precision and saluted. It was the senior messenger, Mubenga.

'Well, Jacob?'

The D.C. did not move, but looked at the dark heavy face with its alert and penetrating eyes. Jacob was a good messenger and he knew his people. There was a moment of silence while the man

149

assembled his thoughts into presentable English for the European officers.

'It is Nkomeshya, sir, the clerk. He is very sick, very sick. He wants you.'

The D.C. nodded.

'He's worse?'

'Yes, sir, much worse.'

Slowly the white man got to his feet. The cadet quickly got up, putting down his unfinished drink.

'Go and wait at the house, Jacob,' the messenger was told. 'I shall come in a few moments. I think Mr Petrie will come, too.'

He turned to look at the cadet, raising an eyebrow and smiling with a hint of derision in his expression. John Petrie felt himself blush.

'Yes, yes, I'll come,' he said hurriedly.

'Good.'

The D.C., Roland Clayton, sat down again.

'Time to finish our drinks,' he said, 'and give Jacob a chance to get back ahead of us.'

They sipped in silence. Presently Clayton got up again.

'Let's go,' he said quietly, and stepped out into the darkness.

Away from the house it was not so dark, though the moon had not yet risen above the trees across the river. They could see the brick path easily and beyond it the narrow road that led past the boma and into the compound. A dog scuttled away before them as they approached the huts. Here and there a dim light burned, but no one sat outside and doors were fast shut. There was an air of expectancy about the compound.

The two men moved quietly in the dust through the area to the last house, a rondavel with a new thatch and clean white walls. The door was ajar and a light showed. Under the shallow eaves stood a tall straight figure, the senior messenger.

As they approached, he stepped forward, and made a gesture towards the door. The D.C. nodded, lowered his head, and entered the little house. Petrie followed, his heart beating unaccountably hard and his throat dry. Mubenga came in, too, and stood waiting just inside the door.

150

The room was furnished with a single iron bed, a table, a tall cupboard, and some home-made bookshelves. The little window was closed, but before it stood a tin with a few flowers, now drooping. All eyes turned to the bed.

On it lay a young man, covered up to his chin in a single blanket, patched, but clean. Petrie glanced round in the dim light of the lantern and noticed how clean the whole place was. He looked at Mubenga and saw the messenger watching and he knew that he was the man who had looked after the young clerk.

'I'm sorry to call you, sir,' whispered the sick man. 'I hope you don't mind.'

Clayton sat down on a stool by the bed and looked intently into Nkomeshya's face.

'It's all right. Don't worry. I want you to get well.'

He looked at his hands.

'Tell me, James,' he said. 'You must tell me all you know. Then perhaps we can help.'

Petrie perched awkwardly on the edge of the table. Mubenga stood rigidly at the foot of the bed. Nkomeshya moved his head slowly from side to side on the low pillow.

'I don't know, sir,' he croaked. 'That is why I am so afraid. I have been given the signs, but I don't know what it is I have done.'

The D.C. leaned over him.

'You must know something,' he urged. 'If you are bewitched, there must be something. When we know, we can destroy it.'

The young clerk twisted in his bed and moaned. There was a long silence.

'Perhaps it is the girl,' he whispered at length.

'What girl?'

'There's a girl up the river at Malala. I want to marry her and she wants me.'

He paused, breathed heavily. Perspiration stood out on his face. He went on.

'But her cousin wants her. He's older. He's related to the chief. He's too old for her, but he wants her.'

He paused again.

151

'He told me to keep away,' he gasped. 'He beat her for speaking to me. He told me I'd be sorry if I saw her again.'

The D.C.'s lips formed a tight line.

'And you saw her?'

'Yes, I saw her. We – we – were together.'

Clayton nodded his head.

'At night?'

'Yes, at night. All night.'

Petrie stared, fascinated. Mubenga sucked in a quick breath. Clayton looked at his hands and flexed his fingers thoughtfully.

'Is that all?'

'Yes, bwana, that is all. I swear that is all.'

'Who is the man?'

Nkomeshya's eyes dilated. He said nothing.

'He is called Mapulanda, sir,' came Mubenga's deep voice, 'Josiah Mapulanda. I know him.'

Clayton nodded. Gently he touched Nkomeshya's shoulder.

'Now that we know, we shall do what we can,' he said.

He turned to the messenger.

'Jacob, you will go to Malala at dawn with another messenger, whoever you wish. You will bring Mapulanda here.'

Mubenga saluted.

'I will take Malesu, sir.'

He hesitated, then added 'But tonight I will stay here.'

The D.C. got up.

'Good. Sleep, James. We shall help you. Come on, John, let's go back.'

They walked out. Petrie found he was trembling a little. He shook himself angrily.

'You see,' he said quietly, as they walked back through the compound, 'it's all suggestion.'

'Is it?' was the grim reply and the cadet said no more.

Mubenga left the next day at dawn. It would take him all day to reach Malala, for the only way was by the river in the little barge. Clayton made the duty messenger go to Nkomeshya's house every hour and report on him. He was very low and did not speak. His breathing was shallow and his eyes had sunk deep into his head. Clayton pursed his lips thoughtfully. There was heaviness about the boma and even the children in the compound were scarcely heard. No one but the messenger went near the little house, and he with fear in his eyes.

'I only hope Mubenga is in time,' the D.C. told Petrie, as they sat down just after dusk. The cadet looked about him nervously. He felt the atmosphere. He felt the expectancy. He still told himself stoutly that it was all a matter of psychology. He stared about him and started suddenly. Clayton's rifle stood just by the sitting room door behind them. He had never seen it there before and for some reason he shuddered.

As the moon rose, they still sat, scarcely speaking. Petrie knew they were waiting, but he did not know for what. Suddenly a dog howled, high, mournful. Then it yelped and the yelp spelt terror. Clayton got up sharply.

'We'd better go,' he said.

Petrie did not answer, but he rose, his eyes on the other's face. Clayton lifted the rifle, quietly loaded it, met the cadet's questioning eyes.

'It may be needed,' he said, and led the way out along the brick path.

Again they padded quietly through the compound. The houses were silent. Tonight no lights showed, but twice as they passed huts they heard a faint murmur of voices. Petrie heard the D.C. breathing and glanced at him. His face was tense. He looked searchingly ahead. I wonder what he expects, thought the cadet, I don't like this. He felt cold and his throat was dry. Suddenly Clayton stopped.

They were looking at Nkomeshya's hut about twenty yards away. The door was ajar, but no light showed. From within came the sound of a moaning voice, crying out incoherently. Petrie felt his hair stir. A shiver ran over him.

By the door was a shape, a small dark shape, unidentifiable, but seemingly crouched by the door. As they watched, it seemed to move and Petrie thought he saw a dwarf figure.

'No!' roared the D.C. and his rifle crashed out into the night.

They ran forward to the little house. Petrie placed a hand against the wall and stood outside, peering about him fearfully. There was no sign of anything, only dust and a mark on the white wall where the bullet had grazed it. He felt sick. Slowly he walked into the hut after Clayton.

The messenger on guard lay seemingly unconscious just inside the door. The D.C.'s hands trembled as he lit the lamp. The soft light brought more normality to the place.

Nkomeshya sat half upright in his bed, his body pressed back against the hard iron frame at the head. His hands clutched the sides of the bed. His eyes were shut.

'James!' said Clayton, sharply.

Slowly the young man's eyes opened. He looked first at the open door, then slowly around. He breathed deeply.

'Sir,' he whispered. 'Sir, it is gone!'

'What? Who?'

Nkomeshya blinked.

'I am not sick,' he replied more strongly, 'it is gone.'

Mubenga arrived the following evening just as they were leaving the boma. The sun was still up and the river flowed bright and clear. The compound was all activity. Nkomeshya sat on a chair outside his hut, talking to the messenger who had stayed with him all day.

The senior messenger came slowly up from the landing, Malesu following and carrying something wrapped in a piece of canvas from the barge. The D.C. looked swiftly at the two men and at the barge.

'Where is Mapulanda?' he demanded sharply.

'He is dead, sir,' replied Mubenga gravely.

'Dead!'

'Yes, sir. We found him and kept him in his house, but in the night he cried out, got up from his bed, and fell by the door. When we picked him up, he was dead.'

'How? Was he sick?'

'No, sir. I think it was his heart.'

Clayton nodded.

'What have you there?' he asked.

Mubenga motioned Malesu to open the canvas. Slowly he lifted out a wooden figure, perhaps eighteen inches high. The cadet peered, fascinated. He knew what it was, a witch-doctor's doll, the doll they said walked at night. It was painted black. The legs

154

and arms were short, the arms stiffly at the sides. The mouth was open. The face was leering, vicious.

Clayton pointed in silence. The figure was split just below the neck. Something had passed right through it and left a jagged exit. The splitting looked new. It could have been a bullet, Petrie thought, and shivered.

'I found this in his house, sir,' said Mubenga, 'he kept it under his bed.'

He looked straight into the D.C.'s eyes and added,

'But the hole was not there, when I saw it yesterday.'

'No,' said Clayton, in an odd voice, 'I don't suppose it was.'

He turned to look at the cadet.

'It might be a matter of psychology,' he said quietly. 'That's what they say it is.'

The cadet said nothing.

The Leopardess

It came from some far place, came like the breath of a strange wind, stealing up quietly, so that it was there before anyone noticed it. There was uneasiness in the still of the evening for a day or two and the villagers looked about them, not quite sure what it was they sensed. But like animals in their instinct they who dwelt out there in the bush knew there was something strange. They knew a presence had come among them.

It was the schoolchildren who told them about it first. They had seen it once, as they came through the trees and down the track past the hard grey outcrop that showed out among the green of the hill. They had seen it just for a moment and fled screaming into the village.

Mwape had been among the villagers who had gathered round the terrified children and stared up the hill towards the rocks. They could see nothing, only the stunted trees and the track and the grey shapes of the rocks. But when the children had calmed and the noise quieted, they heard the cough, deep and sinister, away up there beyond the brow of the hill. The villagers looked at one another and, as the dusk fell with all its tropical speed, they built up the fires by their huts and drove their fowls and goats into shelter.

Mwape could not understand why a leopard should come so near. They were not animals to seek company. They stalked and killed, but rarely near a village. Carefully, he put down the long spear he was sharpening and gazed about the village. It was still and the blue smoke rose straight up from the fires and, in some places, through the dark, untidy thatch of the roofs. The huts clustered close and even now, days afterwards, the people were uneasy. A leopard is no fool.

For some days they neither saw nor heard it, but the children were afraid of their three mile walk to school and no one insisted that they should go. The headman squatted by his hut, chewed, and spat into the dust before him. He was old and he was sick. The people tended their gardens, but never alone, and the girls went down to the river in groups and did not sing and laugh.

Mwape poked the fire with his foot and stared up the hill. As the light faded, he thought he saw a movement and he touched his spear gently. We are bound by fear, he thought, we are many against one beast, but we are bound by fear. Something must be done. He looked into the fire and saw the blue lights flicker above the red heart of it. Behind him his wife murmured to the baby in the hut. His son, Elias, talked to himself in there, too, with the calm assurance of a boy of five. As the night fell, he heard the cough, some way off, but clear, heavy, in the still air. The village fell silent about him and people stood to look away towards the rocks. The leopard was still there.

There were not many young men in the village. Nowadays they all walked the fifty miles to the township and then made their way to the city with its lights and its money and its brazen girls. But Mwape had stayed because his mother was old. In any case he knew the bush, but he feared the town; he saw how changed were the young men who came back from it. He heard their tales and their boasts and he stayed.

He knew now that he was the one. It was he who must find the beast and lift the cloud from the village. He knew and he was afraid. He clenched his hands and rose to walk slowly and uneasily to the headman's hut. Simwanza nodded and spat and said little, but his eyes showed that he was grateful that his problem had been solved for him. Mwape had taken a burden from his shoulders.

156

Vignettes

Mwape spent three days wandering cautiously about the bush below the rocks and along the track that led past them. He saw the traces he expected and his scalp stirred when he smelt the feral odour that clung near the rocks. He did not know how he knew, but his heart said this was a leopardess. There was no evidence, no explanation: he just knew. And he was right.

On the fourth day, spear in hand, watched fearfully by a handful of villagers, he walked to the rocks at dusk and stood to listen. The wind stirred the trees gently and the grass hissed. Then it paused and beyond the rocks he heard not the menacing cough, but a softer, more intimate growling. He knew what the sound meant, a cub and its mother. For some strange reason the leopardess had a cub with it behind the rocks. He walked back down the track, his head lowered, his brows together in a frown. 'Why?' he thought, 'why should it come here with a cub?' The beasts sought far places with their young, but here it was, this creature, right above the village. Back there he said nothing, for this was his problem, his task, and the villagers asked no questions, only watched and waited.

I shall have the cub, he told himself, it will make a small skin for Elias and he will be proud. The headman can have the mother's skin, but I shall have the cub. And still he said nothing, told no one what he knew.

Two days later the beast stood in the half light of the late evening and gazed down on a village that fell silent before it. Witchcraft, they murmured, this is a devil. But Mwape told himself it was not. He watched the beast for the few moments it stood there and something stirred him to admiration. There was a magnificence in the way the leopardess stood, a proud contempt of the fearful village huddled below her. But he still wanted the cub's pelt; he still knew he had to lift fear from the village.

From that night he planned and watched and waited. He saw the beast twice even by day as he prowled about, just a glimpse of sleek smoothness and terrible power, and he could smell where it had been. He took his time now and ventured nearer and nearer to the tangle of rocks that rose among the trees to the right of the track. No one used the track now, except him. They were afraid. So was he, but he had to go beyond the gardens and the river.

157

A few days later he saw the cub, a beautiful animal, still very small, but he saw that it was lame. That is why, he thought, that is why they are here. The little one is injured and the mother guards it until it can move on. Perhaps they will go, he thought, and I have only to wait. He looked back towards the village and saw the smoke of the fires and heard the stillness, the stillness of fear. His pride surged up again. I must kill, he murmured, and the cub shall be mine.

· He found the cleft in the rocks where the cub rested. He saw it from a distance, but he could see the cub rolling in the sunlight. He crept nearer round the base of a great face of rock thirty feet sheer above him. 'Is it now?' he thought and gripped his spear tighter. As he moved something impelled him to look upwards and outlined against the sky he saw the sleek head, the flattened ears. The leopardess was watching him.

He hesitated, moved back to the trees below, and waited. Up there the great eyes never lost him, while away to the right the cub stopped its rolling and clambered up towards its mother. There was still sunlight, fading now, but still clear, and by it he saw that the cub had a gash on its leg, a healing gash. 'They will go,' he said aloud and saw the mother tense at the murmur of his voice.

'Elias shall have the cub,' he said aloud again. 'They shall not go.' But the leopardess answered him with a low growl that seemed to whisper among the trees all about him. He watched the cub vanish among the rocks higher up and he began to creep round, further away now, back in the thicker bush where perhaps he might not be seen, back where he could no longer see the great rock and the head that showed above it.

Presently he came round near the track at the far side of the rocks and, as he peered, he saw the leopardess slink quietly across to a point directly above the track. He could not yet see the cub. Cautiously he edged nearer and his thumb felt the blade of his spear. It was sharp and true, but the light was just beginning to fade now and it was time to act. He moved again, nearer yet to the track, nearer yet to the rocks. And he saw the cub.

It was following its mother across the top of a rock some fifteen feet above him, scrambling awkwardly, and, even as he watched, it fell. It fell about eight or ten feet on to a sloping ledge right beside the track and twenty yards from where he crouched. It is mine, he exulted, and edged nearer, clearing his arm for the throw. As he moved the growl reached him as it had done before, all about him. He glanced up and saw the leopardess crouched, tensed, smooth and magnificent, ready to leap those feet down upon him, if his arm moved with the spear. Only then did he realise he had but one spear.

He sank back into the grass. 'One spear,' he murmured, 'and that must kill the mother first. But she is too far away.' He waited, staring at the cub, conscious that the leopardess remained crouched, ready. The cub was aware now of the danger, too, and crouched, its little teeth bared, its eyes upon him. A rock, he thought, I can kill it with a rock and the mother will come near enough for my spear. Slowly he let his eyes wander and there a few yards to the right was a sharp piece of rock, heavy enough to kill. As he reached for the stone he wanted, he heard the voice.

It was Elias' voice, his son, the child, coming up the track, calling his name, and the path lay directly below where the leopardess still crouched. His heart bounded and he gripped his spear. The jagged stone he had lifted to hurl at the cub fell from his hand and he leapt to his feet. As he did so, the child appeared round the bend in the track, trotting, calling his name plaintively. Mwape sprang on to the track. The leopardess leapt lightly down from the top of the rock, virtually between him and the boy and Elias saw it.

'Stand!' said Mwape sharply, and Elias halted, paralysed, his eyes on the sleek form that stood only a few yards away.

Mwape watched the animal, the sweat pouring down his back, his heart thundering in his ears. Slowly the beast looked away. It looked at the cub, then at him, then at the child. As it did so, Elias ran, not away, but forward past the animal to him and clutched his leg. He stood, his spear raised, but the leopardess did not move. It had not moved as the child ran past it, only watched him. Its eyes never left him, but it made no move to spring.

Mwape leaned down slightly, desperately trying to disengage the little boy's grip and, as he struggled to do so, he met the eyes of the leopardess. They were different; the terrifying savagery had gone. In that moment something passed between them – he did not know what. They looked deep into each other's eyes for long seconds, the man and the beast. For that brief moment they understood each other.

Then suddenly the leopardess turned, unhurriedly, and began to shepherd her cub away, away from the rocks, away into the bush. She did not even look back. He knew she would not return. Mwape half raised his arm as if to throw, then lowered his spear slowly to the ground. He sank on one knee beside the child, one hand on the little shoulder, and Elias found his voice at last.

'It had a cub,' he whispered, 'but you did not throw.'

Mwape ran a hand over his face. His fingers trembled.

'No,' he whispered back. 'No, I did not throw.'

His voice sank lower. 'But I have you,' he added slowly.

They both looked across to where the leopardess had vanished and they were very still.

9

The Final Analysis

It is now a little short of thirty years since I left Africa and sufficient time has elapsed to enable me to achieve some sort of perspective. At this distance in time it becomes possible for me to examine feelings and impressions more dispassionately and yet, because I made such use of personal diaries and of things written at the time, without losing the touch of the actual moment. Hindsight always colours what one says and does about past events to some extent, but in this account of our days in Africa I think a reasonable balance has been kept. And so now it is possible to ask what we gained from Africa, what lasting effects it had upon us. I can say without hesitation that it left a mark on all of us, a mark that will never disappear.

Our years there helped us to understand at least some of the people to a considerable degree. We know something of how Africans think; we understand their failure to see democracy as we see it; we know they are not 'just like us, only black'. We can also understand the fears and the efforts of white South Africans to preserve their way of life and their anger at people thousands of miles away telling them, in complete ignorance, what they ought to be doing. We can see the great contribution the colonial period made to Africa's development, despite what some people want to believe, those who cannot yet grasp that nothing is all bad or all good. The posturing by both black and white people goes on for political and personal ends, for power, but in their hearts most of them know the truth. It is just not expedient to admit it. We came away from Africa knowing a great deal more about its people and about both sides of the problems that beset them.

We also recognised that we had begun – and I repeat, begun – to understand them.

Looking back, we must also give some thought to what we were able to give to Africa and what impact we made, if any at all. There is again no doubt that some impression was made, albeit only a small one, but those small impacts made by each expatriate officer, his wife and even his children all added up, so that overall the European effect was strong; especially when one adds the effect of non-government people, in the mines, in the commercial world, and in the academic world of universities. I like to think that somewhere in what became Zambia there were a few Africans who silently thanked me for some little way in which I had helped them. Our contribution was long hours spent year after year furthering the cause of education by way of inspection, guidance, office work, organisation; much of which would not bear fruit until after we had left the particular area, or even after we had left the territory. For us in the colonial service, that work was done to hasten our own elimination and leave the African to carry forward his own destiny thereafter, although we did not actually think of that aspect very often. The matters in hand were usually too immediate, too pressing, for us to look years ahead. We did that in development plans, but there was always so much on hand, so much to be done – now! But we each left our little mark as one tiny element of the great body of expatriates, and especially that of the colonial service.

But over it all looms Africa itself, the land and its teeming non-human life, the power that lies in nature there, the sheer size of the land which can absorb everything that man can put there. I made an effort to express my feeling about Africa in an article I wrote years after we had left there, and when I had had time to think about all that I had heard and seen and done there. This article follows as a final word on my experience of Africa and what must no doubt be the experience of many others who have lived and worked there.

The Spell of Africa
A spell is cast. Perhaps it is witchcraft, for Africa is the home of witchcraft, so they say, and no one who has been there will deny

it. A lot of unexplainable things happen, and after a year or two there one finds oneself interested in what the witch-doctor says and does. Strangely enough what he predicts so often turns out to be right and that seems to happen too frequently to be mere coincidence. But witchcraft is not all evil, and some of the spells cast in Africa are cast by simple people far from the growing frenzy of life in the cities, a life that is trying to make up for centuries in a few short years. The real spirit of Africa, the Africa that speaks without words, lies not in the cities, but far away, amid the hills and the trees and the grasses, away where the animals still roam free and people do not use clocks to regulate their day. Out there one can travel a hundred miles – they still talk miles in Africa – and see nobody, perhaps nothing, not even an animal: only the limitless bush, the short trees, the tall grasses, the grey rocks, the concealing scrub, and, above, the sky which always seems vaster and more blue, and yet somehow closer.

The real Africa is where the black population lives and has lived for untold centuries. It is not in the far north, which has long been Arab country, though the Arabs, too, are invaders, interlopers, like the Europeans. It is not in the far south, which for long years lay virtually uninhabited, until the white men needed it to help them on their route to India and the East. When the Portuguese and the Dutch and the British were gaining a foothold round the Cape, the rugged, vigorous Bantu peoples were moving down from the north, each tribe pushing aside another in turn. Amid all this upheaval, the quiet, peaceful, indigenous people moved out of the way, into the remote bush and the swamps and the desert. The remnants of them still live there.

Almost everywhere one goes away from the main roads in Africa south of the Sahara, life goes on as it has done for a thousand years and more, stirring to the morning sun, the faint breeze shaking the dew from the leaves and rustling the long grass so that the drinking buck lift their heads, startled, ready for flight, and the elephant flaps his great ears slowly and wends his way back deliberately from the river to the cool shade of the trees to stand almost invisible, gently swinging his trunk. By the time the sun is over the far horizon across the endless treetops, there is no animal to be seen. They have all slipped away to the peace and secrecy of the

163

places in the bush that only they know, only they can find.

In the villages on such mornings, the blue smoke hangs lazily over the dark thatch of the rondavels and there are already the shrill cries of women drawing water from the river or the well. They startle the birds and send the last scavenging hyena slinking back into the bush. Presently a chattering line of men, women, and children curls out from the village for maybe a mile, maybe more or less, to the mealie patch or the cassava garden. In some places the long, shallow canoes, dug from a single tree trunk, nose out on to the river, watched by the silent crocodiles, with only the eyes and the tips of their snouts visible above the water, and the noisy, uninhibited hippo, snorting and blowing in abandon. Sometimes a hippo will chase a canoe and nudge it, tipping its occupants into the water and then swimming off, making noises that sound almost like laughter. The crocodile has no sense of humour; it waits and watches for the unwary, whether man or beast. With the crocodile, the cost of carelessness is death.

Until the sun is high, the village is still, at first sight quite deserted, until some slight movement in a dark doorway shows that someone is there; an old man, dreaming of the days gone by, spitting casually into the dry, beaten earth beyond the shadow of the hut, letting time go by, because now he can do little else but let time go by. Not even the children are about. The older ones, old enough to walk maybe five or seven or ten miles, have set out, perhaps even before it was fully light, on their journey to school at a larger village several miles away. The little ones are with their mothers, on their backs all day; or, if they can walk, toddling round the edge of the garden, while their mothers and fathers and aunts and uncles work and sing and chatter. It seems to be only in the towns that Africans are silent, sullen and gloomy, and even there their natural light-heartedness often breaks through in singing and laughter.

The day passes, slowly, but time does not matter out there and, as the sun slants down, that line of people comes curling back again, the women's voices still high and shrill, laughing, arguing, calling their children, while the babies are the quietest ones I have ever heard; noise seems to come from the children only when they have reached the age to run about, play, and fight, when their voices are really heard. The women usually arrive back before the men and very soon the fires glow and the smoke drifts over the village, out over the huts and the surrounding bush, and over the men as they in turn come trudging in, more quietly, but with a dignity about them, a dignity that they seem to lose in the towns and their modern ways. Perhaps it is because here they are at home, at one with their surroundings. The bush speaks to them, whereas the town does not.

Most of Africa has its seasons: for the most part just two of them, the wet and the dry. The wet season is short and, as a rule, violent; with deluges of rain, thunder that always seems to roll directly overhead, and brilliant, often terrifying lightning, which seems to be personally seeking out the watcher. Half an hour, an hour, two hours, sometimes more, and the storm passes on, leaving a bright sky flecked with clouds and everything steaming in the sun, really steaming, so that for a few minutes one is surrounded by mist. The dry season is long and cool and infinitely peaceful, apart from the occasional windy day. Everything – people, animals, birds, plants – is geared to meet the dryness that will last for six months or more before the next rain comes, when more rain will fall in three months than in a whole year in temperate climates. Somehow the trees keep their leaves, brown and dusty though they often may be. Sometimes new growth appears just before the first rain, tiny green shoots amid the brown grass, more vivid on patches that have been burnt. The small buck love these green shoots. On the trees the new leaves are red; to Europeans, a sort of autumn in reverse that gives a very special character to the African bush.

Where there are great rivers, especially where the Zambesi flows, the wet season has created flood plains year after year for centuries, great sheets of water that often make the river twenty miles wide for a time. Grass grows up through the water, until maybe half of the expanse of water is hidden under its greenness, so that the ground looks solid. When the dry weather returns, the water retreats, the river shrinks back to its normal width, and the plain is left rich with good silt and ready for use. And very good use of it is made by the village farmers. Many villages have wet and dry season sites, the people moving back and forth as the seasons change, although it is a recognised tradition that no one moves before the paramount chief of the area makes his migration.

Africa impresses by its silence when one stands far from the main roads, but it is a silence that is not really silence. One has only to stand and listen for a few moments and gradually, even in the middle of the day when many creatures are stilled by the heat of the sun, one will hear so many sounds, none of them loud and all of them seemingly distant. By day nothing seems to move near at hand. Movement always seems to happen far away, beyond those anthills or in that distant clump of stunted trees. Perhaps it is this silence which is not really silence that makes the night in Africa so magnificent and eloquent.

To begin with, there is no moon like an African moon: huge, glowing, alive. There is no sky as velvet deep and eloquently silent, when one stands on the edge of the village and looks and listens. Africa is one of the few places where one can actually see by starlight. But if the moon is up, and it seems to be up more in Africa than anywhere else, then one can see much more. Back there in the village one hears the sound of voices, always quieter once darkness falls, and sees the glow of the fires, glowing embers without flames. The voices carry clearly in the darkness, no longer raucous or shrill. All argument seems to die with the going down of the sun and the villagers are at peace with their surroundings and with one another. Whatever has gone on in the daylight hours, there seems to be a kind of truce, at least until the sun rises again.

The listener knows the sounds from the village, recognising what each one means, visualising what is happening back there. But out ahead, in the bush, the sounds are often unfamiliar and cannot be recognised, the faint sounds of the life that stirs in the darkness, the life that brings terror to some, human and animal alike: the crack of a branch, the swish of the long grass, the soft rustle of feet, the swirl of the water in the river. When the moon is high, dim shapes can be seen, softly and slowly wending their way down to the river and back again, for this is the time for drinking after the long dry day, when an animal can become almost as parched as the land itself. The elephants, the lions, the leopards, the antelopes, all will go there as soon as it grows dark enough or, perhaps, light enough to see without being seen easily in return. The twilight and the moonlight and the dawn light give them what they want. There will be the occasional cry, but the life of the bush has long since learned to be silent, whether in making an attack or in escaping it. Most of the noises heard are those of soft movement. Here and there the gleam of eyes in the darkness shows that something is watching the village: the hyenas watch because they are Africa's born scavengers; the leopards watch for possible prey and because they are wary; the lions pause to look in lofty disdain as they pass.

In Africa, perhaps the night speaks most eloquently of all. It speaks of the vastness, and of the unchanged life of man and beast. It touches you and leaves a mark which can be felt, but not seen. It weaves a spell of Africa that calls to the corners of the earth, so that he who has been there and lived there always wants to go back, not to the towns and their bustle and their shallow modernity, but to the bush, to the great silence that is not really silence. It is magic, but not black magic. It is a spell that binds, yet one never wishes to break free.

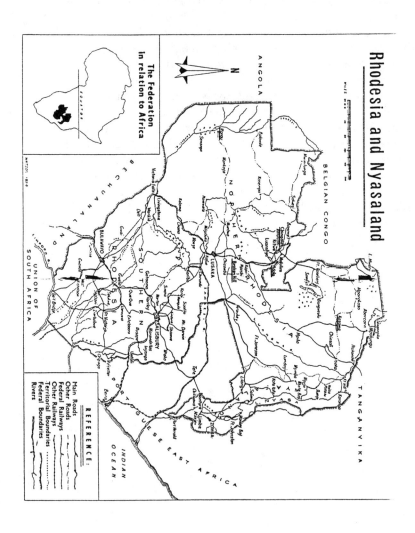

Rhodesia and Nyasaland

The Federation in relation to Africa

REFERENCE:
Main Roads
Other Roads
Federal Railways
Other Railways
Territorial Boundaries
Federal Boundaries
Rivers

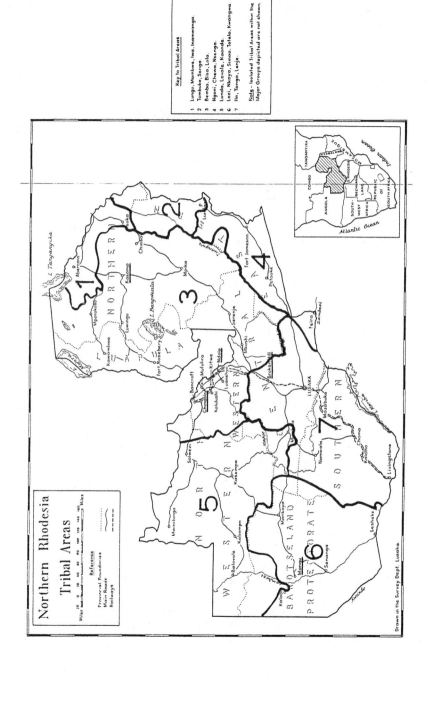

Northern Rhodesia
Tribal Areas

Miles 20 0 20 40 60 80 100 120 140 160 Miles

Reference

Provincial Boundaries ....
Main Roads _____
Railways ___ ___ ___

Drawn in the Survey Dept. Lusaka.

Key to Tribal Areas

1 Lungu, Mambwe, Iwa, Inamwanga.
2 Tumbuka, Senga.
3 Bemba, Bisa, Lala.
4 Ngoni, Chewa, Nsenga.
5 Lunda, Lovale, Kaonde.
6 Lozi, Nkoya, Simaa, Totela, Kwangwa.
7 Ila, Tonga, Lenje.

Note - Isolated Tribal Areas within the
Major Groups depicted are not shown.

9

Index and glossary

170

Index and glossary

people, by far the best way to see the animals in their natural state without unduly alerting or alarming them. Nsefu and Luambe were the largest and best-appointed camps. Pages 109, 110, 115.

Lundazi Castle hotel: A lavish structure built by a district commissioner, originally an office and dwelling but for many years now a hotel. Pages 112, 113.

Lusaka: The Northern Rhodesian and, since independence, the Zambian capital. Page 82.

Makishi: Masked dancers who performed on all ceremonial occasions, especially in Barotseland. Page 72.

Monckton Commission: A body formed in London by the imperial government to report on the development and future of Northern Rhodesia. Pages 82, 83.

Mongu: The administrative and commercial centre of Barotseland. Pages 48, 56, 59, 61, 62, 68, 70, 75, 76.

Mtwara: The specially built port for the East African Groundnut Scheme, which unfortunately failed. Page 9.

Muoyo: The senior wife of the paramount chief of Barotseland. Page 70.

Nalikwanda: The Lozi royal barge, used only by the paramount chief, all the paddlers being lesser chiefs or *indunas*. Pages 69, 70.

Ndola: The main town of the Western Province of Northern Rhodesia. Developed when copper was first exploited, it later became the main commercial and distribution centre for the whole Copperbelt area as the mining moved further north. Pages 26, 27, 28, 29, 38, 40, 43, 81.

Northern Province: The largest province in Northern Rhodesia, now Zambia, bordering on Zaire and Tanzania. Page 98.

Nyika plateau: The highest land area in Northern Rhodesia, lying across the Tanzanian border in the far north-east corner and reaching over seven thousand feet. It is notable for its rocky outcrops and lack of trees. Pages 98, 113.

O.C.T.U.: The Officer Cadet Training Unit, training prospective officers for the army. There were two such units in New Zealand during the war. Page 4.

Salisbury: Now called Harare, the capital of Zimbabwe, formerly Southern Rhodesia. Pages 10, 90.

Sinoia caves: An interesting cave system, about eighty miles north-west of Harare (formerly Salisbury). The caves are similar to and yet distinctly different in many ways from those at Waitomo in New Zealand or at Jenolan in Australia. Page 91.

Index and glossary

Southern Rhodesia: A self-governing British colony from 1924 after a plebiscite conducted in 1923. It was part of the Central African Federation while that body existed and is now the independent state of Zimbabwe. Pages 21, 23.

Stephenson, J. E.: A B.S.A. Company assistant collector and surveyor, known to all as Chirupula. Page 26.

UNIP: The United National Independence Party, the main political party in Zambia, came into existence while Zambia was still Northern Rhodesia and is still the major party. Kenneth Kaunda was one of its founder members. Pages 85, 94, 118, 119, 129.

Vlei: An open stretch of land in the bush, also called a pan, often a shallow lake in the wet season. Page 99.

V.S.O.: The Volunteer Service Overseas, an organisation based in the United Kingdom, which sent young people overseas to assist in various government departments in British colonies and protectorates. They were usually sent for a year between leaving school and commencing university studies. A considerable number were sent to Education in Northern Rhodesia. Pages 117, 118, 119.

Western Samoa: An island group in the Pacific. A New Zealand mandate after World War I and later a Trust Territory, it achieved independence in 1962. Pages 128, 130.

Witch-doctors: Men of spiritual influence in many Third World countries, sometimes malignant but also often expert herbalists and medicine men. They are particularly numerous and influential among the black races of Africa. Pages 133, 134.

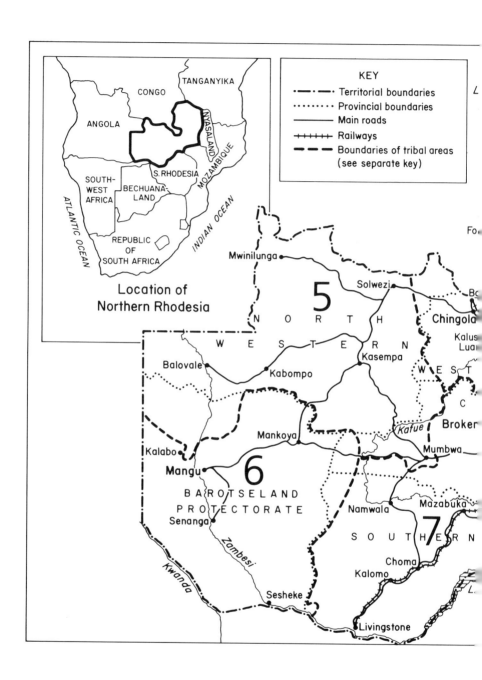

KEY
Territorial boundaries
Provincial boundaries
Main roads
Railways
Boundaries of tribal areas
(see separate key)

Location of
Northern Rhodesia